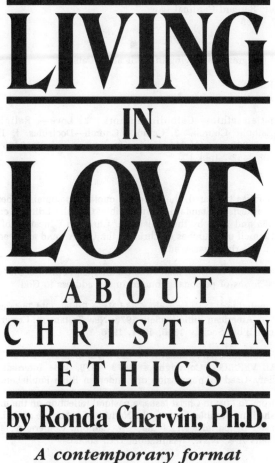

LIVING
IN
LOVE

ABOUT
CHRISTIAN
ETHICS

by Ronda Chervin, Ph.D.

*A contemporary format
leading up to perennial truths*

St. Paul Books & Media

Nihil obstat: Rev. Msgr. Richard K. Malone, S.T.D.
Imprimatur: Bernard Cardinal Law
October 7, 1988

Library of Congress Cataloging-in-Publication Data

Chervin, Ronda.
  Living in love.

     1. Christian ethics—Catholic authors. 2. Love— Religious
aspects—Catholic Church. 3. Catholic Church—Doctrines. I. Title.
BJ1249.C34 1988   241'.042   88-18485
ISBN 0-8198-4452-7 (pbk.)

Printed in the United States of America

The Daughters of St. Paul
50 St. Paul's Ave., Boston, MA 02130

The Daughters of St. Paul are an international congregation of women
religious serving the Church with the communications media.

1 2 3 4 5 6 7 8 9   95 94 93 92 91 90 89 88

Contents

Why Live in Love?

Most psychologists believe that every human person wants to love and be loved. Many of us have daydreams about great deeds of love and also fantasies about being loved perfectly.

And yet, most of us live selfishly a great deal of the time. Our deeds fall far short of our dreams of generosity, and most of us feel that the love we receive is insufficient or fatally flawed.

Why? Why should there be such a discrepancy between our hopes and our daily experience? Is there any way to bridge the gulf between fantasy and fulfillment?

Put another way—suppose you could read your own tombstone and it said:

Here lies J. Doe—
a life of success in every pursuit
but J. never learned
how to love.

I think that such a summing-up of my own life would be the ultimate failure, and I would guess many readers would agree.

As you can see from glancing at the chapter heads, this book plans to suggest a way of growing in love. I will begin with experiences of love and lack of love in daily life, without much explicit reference to God. Then, in the last part of *Living in Love* I will show how a God of Love who reveals himself in Christ and in the Church can help us to reach our goal.

But before proceeding it will be necessary to examine our individual starting points and also to see how love can be defined.

Questions About Love in Your Life

It is suggested that you jot down your answers to these questions and those of subsequent chapters in a notebook numbering it according to the page numbers of this book.

To insure privacy you may want to use code names for people you mention.

1. Think of a person, past or present—someone you have heard about but *not* known personally—who seems very loving to you. Describe this person in a short paragraph.

2. Describe those people you have known personally who seem to you to be most loving.

3. Toward whom have *you* been most loving? Describe an incident of such love on your part.

4. Answering as honestly as possible, how do you rate these goals on a scale of 1-6, with 1 for the highest-rated goal and 6 for the lowest:

fame	monetary success
popularity	independence
peace of mind	being a loving person

Write a few reasons for your priorities or hesitancies.

5. What do you consider to be the main difficulty in your character which causes you to act unlovingly at times?

6. What way do you find most successful for overcoming this difficulty? (Some examples would be self-analysis, talking it over with friends, will power, and prayer.)

(If you are doing this exercise with others in a class or small group, it will be very interesting to share your answers to these six questions with others. Form circles of five people or fewer. Each person may tell about his or her answer to question 1. Then the group may continue with question 2, and so on. The small-circle method of discussion is especially successful, because everyone is called upon to share instead of having three or four talkative people dominating discussion in a large group with the rest remaining relatively passive.)

Your Scorecard on Love

Pick out a day which includes your usual activities and make a scorecard of loving and unloving thoughts, words and deeds, according to your criteria of love, omitting whatever seems neutral. Include as much as you can, all the way from nasty thoughts about drivers on the road to warm fantasies about people you love, from snappish curses to a real "How are you?"—from a slammed door to a swift hug.

The most effective way to make a scorecard is to carry a pad or sheet of paper in your pocket or handbag and make notes on yourself. Naturally it is impossible to capture the millions of little thoughts and deeds that happen in a day. You can limit yourself to ideas that last a minute or more, and words and acts that are deliberate rather than automatic.

Do not decide that your scorecard experiment is invalid if you find yourself purposely doing more good things than usual in order to make the loving column longer. Such "cheating" is also a way to learn—namely, to see how much easier it is to change your habits than you thought!

In such self-examination a factor comes into play which the philosopher Von Hildebrand calls *sanction and disavowel*. Suppose you yell at someone. You can *sanction* that response by thinking to yourself afterwards that the victim of your rage deserved it, or you can *disavow* it by asking forgiveness for losing your temper.

In cases where you *sanction* your response and it is an unloving one, you might make two notations under the column of unloving responses. In cases where you *disavow* a negative response you might put one entry under loving as you ask for forgiveness or regret your words.

Here is a sample of the beginning of a scorecard:

Loving	Unloving
1. Said hello to my roommate.	1. Got angry because she left the breakfast dishes in the sink.
2. Called Sue to see if she needed a ride to work.	2. Added my dishes to the pile in the sink.
3. Prayed for rain to end the drought.	3. Called a stupid driver a name.

Now spend a day working on your scorecard of loving and unloving thoughts, words and deeds. Put a date on the top and set up 2 columns:

Scorecard for _____
                         date

Loving	Unloving
1.	1.
2.	2.
3.	3.
and so on.	and so on.

Reflections on Results

What did you learn from your scorecard? Some of you may have been surprised because there were more loving thoughts, words and deeds than you had anticipated. Some people are very hard on themselves. They are more sensitive to their faults than to their virtues, with the result that they think of their day mainly in terms of their failures in love, neglecting the countless good aspects of their relationships with others. On the other hand, some of you may have been upset to realize how long the unloving column was. Some people think that because they would like to be decent human beings they are very loving, but a scorecard of their daily behavior reveals a predominance of negative responses. Many times this is because a person may be very loving with those to whom he or she is close, but quite hostile to all others. If your scorecard had more unloving than loving entries, do not despair. Today may be the beginning of your transformation.

(These reflections lend themselves to group sharing. Each one could tell of an especially loving and unloving thought, word or deed. The others could describe how they feel when on the receiving end of such words or deeds. Then the causes of such responses could be discussed.)

Your Program
for Becoming More Loving

Find a few hours when you can be alone with a person very close to you or with God. Try to think about the basic elements in your life in terms of loving and unloving patterns. Here are some questions which could help you:

1. What are the main relationships in your life right now?

2. What are the difficult features of each relationship?

3. How do your chief faults contribute to stresses within your daily life?

4. How would analysis, discussion with friends, will power or prayer (or all of these) help you to change negative patterns? For example, would you be less irritable if you got to the root of certain frustrations in your life and tried to do something about them instead of suffering in silence?

Spend some time working out a program for a more loving life in terms of what you have discovered in this period of reflection. This could be done by imagining a typical day in your life and figuring out what new responses you could make—such as greeting people on arising, praying for people instead of judging them, joking instead of cursing, etc. You might try to crystalize your plan in one phrase which summarizes your intention, such as: "Don't hold it in; tell your friends"; or "Let go, let God"; or "Do it yourself; don't make others do it."

Now take a day to practice your new program, keeping another scorecard, labeled:

———————————
date

Loving	Unloving
1.	1.
2. etc.	2. etc.

(In a group share your progress.)

With these personal experiences in mind, you will probably feel a desire to know more about love, and especially how to define it more clearly.

What Is Love?

Which words would you include in a definition of love? Write them in your notebook.

As you read the insights about love which follow, try to see which of them are compatible with your original ideas.

Love Is
a Response to Preciousness

When considering love for people, I find what seems to be the best definition in the writings of the philosopher Dietrich Von Hildebrand: "Love is a response to another person because our hearts are touched by the beauty and preciousness of his or her personality."[1] This concept can be extended to include any other loved beings, such as animals, flowers, trees, music, art or God.

You might now make a list of people and things you especially love.

Think of each being you have noted in your list and reflect on the way in which your love has singled out this person or type of natural or artistic creation, because of your response to the unique preciousness you perceive in it.

(In a group situation each member could describe his or her feelings about different people and things on the list with the others joining in. For example, John says that he loves roses because they are so perfect and their color is so wonderful. Sue adds that her favorite flower is the lily and describes it.)

Von Hildebrand takes exception to the famous idea that "love is blind." Even though infatuated lovers tend to be blind to some faults, it is more true that, far from

---

1. Dietrich Von Hildebrand, *Man and Woman* (Chicago: Franciscan Herald Press, 1965), p. 11.

being blind, the genuine lover sees what most of us are too blunt to notice. Who knows all the special, cute qualities of a baby better—a person who does not like children and thinks all babies look alike, or a father and mother who gaze upon their little one with awe and delight? Who sees more of the true nature of a daisy—the person who steps on it in passing or the one who loves daisies so much that he or she cannot walk by a patch of them without stopping and rejoicing in their beauty?

Love and Delight

There are many different types of love. One of these is what the philosopher Stephen Schwarz has called delight love.[2]

When a person is delighted by someone or something, the main emphasis is on the desire of the lover to enjoy the beloved by contemplation, sight, touch or possession. In delight love it is the lover's joyful response that is in the foreground, rather than the responsibilities of love, which will be described later as characterizing donation love.

Some people identify love so exclusively with deeds that they fail to realize the enormous role that contemplative delight plays in our happiness. Those who love nature may spend some of their happiest hours simply gazing at the ocean, the mountains or their own gardens. A mother spends many delighted moments smiling at her babies as she feeds them. The tender, joyful expression on her face is engraved indelibly in the sensitive memory of the child. Some of the most ecstatic moments of lovers are not in the dark but in the light, as eyes full of love meet and stare in amazement, seeing their own love mirrored in each other's glance.

---

2. Much of the following sections on delight love and donation love has been derived from: Stephen Schwarz, *Love: Some Philosophical and Practical Thoughts*, University of Rhode Island.

Within the next few days, spend some time in contemplative delight of a loved person or anything else you find beautiful. With a person this can be done by looking directly into his or her eyes in silence or quiet conversation. Immerse yourself in the preciousness of the other, giving yourself time to experience how your love unifies you with that goodness. Rejoice and give thanks. Describe some of your experiences in your notebook.

A traditional name for the type of love which seeks to possess the beloved is *eros*. In ancient Greece the word eros comprised not only sexual desire but any kind of longing for a being who could fulfill the lover in some way. Eros was the word for the love of beauty and of the divine as well as for sexual passion. The famous philosopher Plato (427-347 B.C.) describes love as a kind of madness, sometimes foolish, but sometimes divine. (See Plato's dialogue, the *Phaedrus*.) A person who normally leads a rather humdrum or conformist existence is knocked off his or her feet by the passion of love. For the first time, perhaps, something besides one's own self-centered plans becomes really important. Instead of beginning the day with the question of how to solve problems efficiently and working out enjoyable ways to relax, the lover constantly thinks about the beloved— where is he or she? Is my loved one happy? When can I see him or her?

Have you ever had such an experience of love? What do you remember most about it?

Love and Donation

The lover may respond to the preciousness of another with delight, but there is another theme of love which is certainly just as important: responsibility and care. Love mobilizes energy for protection, assistance, and even sacrifice of life, in the interest of preserving what is deemed precious. The more you love a person, part of nature or your country, the more you want to donate yourself to promoting its welfare. The admiring judgment, "She would do anything for a person in need," does not refer to *delight* love, but to what Schwarz calls *donation* love.

Sometimes, as Schwarz points out, donation love reaches beyond delight love. A nurse may have to care for a patient who is very disagreeable, but if her donation love is great enough she will overcome her natural reactions to the sick person's ungrateful behavior in order to help him or her get well. In donating herself with love to the cranky patient's needs, the nurse is responding to the preciousness and dignity of the patient as a human being whose worth transcends the situation of the hospital stay.

Another name for donation love is a word that was originally used to describe the special type of love which Christ commanded his followers to show to the suffering: agapic love. Here are some passages from Scripture which describe this type of love.

From the Gospel of St. Matthew (25:31-40):

"When the Son of man comes in his glory, and all the angels with him, then he will sit on his glorious throne. Before him will be gathered all the nations.... Then the King will say to those at his right hand, 'Come, O blessed of my Father, inherit the kingdom prepared for you from the foundation of the world; for I was hungry and you gave me food, I was thirsty and you gave me drink, I was a stranger and you welcomed me, I was naked and you clothed me, I was sick and you visited me, I was in prison and you came to me.' Then the righteous will answer him, 'Lord, when did we see you hungry and feed you....' And the King will answer them, 'Truly, I say to you, as you did it to one of the least of these my brethren, you did it to me.'"

From the First Letter of St. John (4:7-10, 20-21):

"Let us love one another; for love is of God, and he who loves is born of God and knows God. He who does not love does not know God; for God is love. In this the love of God was made manifest among us, that God sent his only Son into the world, so that we might live through him. In this is love, not that we loved God but that he loved us and sent his Son to be the expiation for our sins.

"If any one says, 'I love God,' and hates his brother, he is a liar; for he who does not love his brother whom he has seen, cannot love God whom he has not seen. And this commandment we have from him, that he who loves God should love his brother also."

The apex of donation love consists in the love a person shows to an enemy even to the point of sacrifice. With Christ as the model, we find great people like Martin Luther King able to live by this proclamation, which was composed to give courage to non-violent Blacks faced with persecution to the death by racists: "To our most bitter opponents we say: 'We shall match your capacity to inflict suffering by our capacity to endure suffering. We shall meet your physical force with soul force. Do to us what you will, and we shall continue to love you. We cannot in all good conscience obey your unjust laws, because noncooperation with evil is as much a moral obligation as is cooperation with good. Throw us in jail, and we shall still love you. Bomb our homes and threaten our children, and we shall still love you....' " [3]

In your notebook write a few paragraphs describing examples of donation love which others have shown to you. Instances mentioned need not be as dramatic as those described above; they could involve long-term small sacrifices made for your welfare by a relative or friend.

Now write about your own donation love for others in the past.

---

3. Martin Luther King, Jr., *The Wisdom of Martin Luther King in His Own Words* (New York: Lancer Books, 1968), p. 34.

Are there any situations in your life right now which need donation love from you?

(In a group an enjoyable hour can be spent as follows: Everyone brings in some very meaningful gift received in the past. Each person holds up the gift and describes why it meant so much and passes it around.)

To conclude this introduction to *Living in Love,* here is a list of stages of growth in love. You might want to check areas in which you are deficient and star those in which you excel.

Stages of Growth in Love

1. Love as comfort and warmth received from others. (The baby receiving warmth from parents; children and adults receiving affection from intimate friends, relatives and God.)

2. Love as absorption in impersonal beings, such as color, forms and structures. (This delight in impersonal beings, so characteristic of children, can be stultified if one is too busy for play and contemplation. On the other hand, delight in the impersonal may become an escape from intermingling with people.)

3. Delight in other people.

4. Love of others as *completing* me—friends, lovers, God. (Lonely people experience severe deprivation in this regard. Possessive people emphasize this type of love to the exclusion of others.)

5. Reconciliation love—after conflicts. (Those unwilling to forgive cannot experience this type of love.)

6. Donation love, to help others. (Egocentric people are deficient in this regard.)

7. Gratitude love. (Directed to people and to God. Bearing grudges blinds one to the good received.)

8. Total love. (Responding to the unique preciousness of all others, and giving oneself as an instrument of
love regardless of the cost.)

Hopefully as a result of the preliminary questions
and exercises in this chapter you will want to read on to
explore how the *desire* to be more loving can lead to
actually *becoming* more loving.

Becoming
a Loving Person

How obligated is a human person to follow the path of love rather than the path of egocentricity?

Probably in some ways you would like to commit yourself to the view that you "are your brother's keeper"—that you ought to do everything you can all the time to respond lovingly to others. But there is probably also a part of you which is thinking: "Okay, that's all very nice, but what about me—what about my survival? I'll be glad to help others as much as I can, but I certainly don't feel obligated to do anything which would hurt my own chances of having a good life. Aren't you being a bit idealistic in this book?"

In response to these last questions, I would state that it would be idealistic, in the sense of being unrealistic, to claim that most people are willing to live totally for others, but it is realistic to believe that most people do want to try to work toward the ideal of love, even if they recognize that they may fail very often. Few people would like to be known for their selfishness, even though they might clutch onto egocentric goals at times of desperation and despair.

To realize how *unselfish* you are, consider the following:

If you were offered a guarantee of lifelong happiness with the proviso that you must do any one of the following things, which ones would you refuse to do (cross them off if you would refuse):

    a) torture an innocent human being
    b) murder an innocent human being
    c) maim a child
    d) cause an innocent friend to go to jail for life
    e) be a spy for an evil group of people who are enslaving one hundred innocent individuals
    f) rape someone
    g) earn your living by setting up a slave system.

Which of the following acts would you avoid because you think they are unloving, even though you would have furthered your goals by doing them:

    1) cheat a person who needed the money
    2) pretend to love someone in order to get into a set of people who could help your career
    3) tell someone you love him or her when you don't, because that person is in love with you and would have sexual relations with you if she or he thought you were really in love
    4) to avoid complications, leave a person hurt in an accident which was your fault

The philosopher Von Hildebrand describes ethics in terms of what he calls "due response." There is a certain response due to the dignity of a person which makes certain types of treatment immoral. Because a person is precious, I ought to respect this by not treating him or her like an expendable means to my own goals. All the items (a-g) listed above involve failure to respond to the basic goodness of a human being. No human being should be tortured, murdered, maimed, unjustly punished, enslaved or raped. Justice is the minimum requirement of love and care. For this reason no one has a right to pursue his own egocentric happiness by overriding the basic rights of others to which a just response is due. Only in the case of extreme guilt are certain rights abrogated, and even then it must be a last resort—I refer to cases of self-defense and just wars for the defense of nations.

Items 1-4 mentioned above are less dramatic but also involve due response. Human beings are obligated to help and respect each other as much as possible. Such is the due response based on elementary human solidarity as well as loving brotherhood.

The philosopher Martin Buber has formulated his ethics in terms of the distinction between what he calls I-Thou and I-It relationships. In our technological age, we are very much tempted to treat human beings as if they were machines or things: "its" instead of persons— "thou's." I have a rusty old can-opener. I throw it out and get another. No problem. The old can-opener is replaceable. It has no name. It has no feelings. Its value is strictly dependent on the worth that I, the consumer, give to it.

When I cheat a person, pretend to love him or her to get my way, deal with him or her in a prejudiced way, or leave him or her wounded in order to avoid going to traffic court, I am acting as if another human being is but a thing which can be used by me and then replaced by another. I forget that every human being has feelings— that every other person is a center of existence just as I am, with needs and longings and hopes.

On the other hand, according to Buber, I am responding to the "thou" of personhood in another when I realize that he or she is irreplaceable, wonderful and worthy of respect no matter how much in the way of my immediate plans. If I look up at the waiter and smile genuinely, for a second I have acknowledged that he or she is not just a functionary to take care of my desires but a person whose value transcends that situation, a human being of as much worth as I am.

Justice is the minimum of love. We ought to respond to the right of others that "man may not be the victim of man" (motto of the Taizé Community, an ecumenical group fostering love in the world).

Yet no matter how much we may agree on certain basic evils we hope we'd never commit, there is a very good reason why we still do not live in love as much as we could. It is because we all have some flaws or even vices which are ingrained in our characters and which lead to the negation of love in daily relationships.

In this chapter we are going to describe some very common faults to see how they run counter to the response of love that is due. To make it interesting I will give short narratives and also have you write your own.

Manipulation vs. Respect

Here are some possible thoughts of a shrewd manipulator:

"Why do I manipulate people so much? Simple. Because they're so stupid! They have no idea of what's really best for them. They just muddle along, pressured by all kinds of unconscious tendencies and societal trends, never thinking out for themselves what would really change things for the better. But I do know what would be best and I've studied their characters well enough to know how to push a few buttons at the right moment so that they agree without even thinking about it.

"I think it began when I was a little girl and my mother told me that the way to get around Dad was to wait to ask him a favor until he was comfortably resting in his recliner after dinner. It always worked! Now it's second nature. There's nothing malicious about it really, because I don't actually hurt anyone. I just bring people around to realizing how good my own well-thought-out plans really are.

"Why get involved with unpleasant confrontation scenes when, with a little adroit flattery, you can work behind the scenes and get the results you want? Why shouldn't I be gleeful when long-hatched plans come to fruition?"

The dictionary gives this meaning of manipulation: "to manage or control artfully or by shrewd use of influence, especially in an unfair or fraudulent way." The use of the words "shrewd" or "unfair" rule out the looser popular definition, which includes any kind of skillful management of human affairs for the good.

Can you, the reader, think of any examples of manipulation you practice or have watched others practice? Write your answer in your notebook.

From many experiences of *being* manipulated people may become cynical or withdrawn. Here are some thoughts a victim of manipulation might have:

"I've practically become a hermit since arriving on this scene. At first I was naive and trusted people but now I realize that everyone has an angle. Just you watch! By the second time you meet someone, you'll find out that they are planning to use you in some way as a 'contact,' or an 'ally,' someone to borrow money or a car from—whatever.

"It's so disappointing. Every time I think there's an exception, the real truth comes out...my feelings are being manipulated for someone else's gain. For example, I thought X was my real friend. I did everything for her. I lent money to her, let her use my car, spent hours talking about her problems, and then it came out that the whole thing was a plan to get to know my brother!

"I just don't believe in people anymore. My dog is the only sincere being I know. I can do without those cheery, phony smiles, stupid invitations, and other human pretenses—everyone's an egotist if you scratch the surface."

How do you, the reader, feel when you think you have been manipulated?

I believe that the opposite of manipulation is not passive stupidity but rather a deep attitude of respect for others.

Here is a description of a person having this kind of reverent attitude:

"I never knew what the word reverent meant in connection with a response to a human being until I met Cathy. Just the way she looks at a person—a sort of piercing sweetness—not the dull, infuriating lamblike submission some good people have—is something really different.

"The way she looks at me when I'm being phony—it's as if she can see right through the manipulative shrewdness to the anxious fear in my heart. Her eyes overflow with compassion and she seems to feel the hurt in me that I've long covered over with stoical bravado.

"That special respectful look on Cathy's face has no judging quality in it. It's as if she sees a 'me' which is so good that even the awful 'me' when I'm at my worst, cannot hide its glory.

"She never mixes into my life with little hints, pushing and pulling, and concealed manipulation. But even though I see her only occasionally, I feel that her friendship is always there in the background—like lovely music in the distance. And if I come to her for advice, it's as if she's been studying me for years. She knows just what questions to ask to help me see what's the best way to go.

"I used to think that I was the only one to appreciate what a marvelous friend she was. Then she had an accident and had to be in the hospital—there must have been fifty people there in one week caring about her."

Have you ever known anyone with this virtue of respect for others?

There are many reasons why some of us are manipulative rather than reverent. On the surface there is the desire to get one's own way, to seem "sharper" than others or to avoid being viewed as a passive "pushover."

Deeper causes may involve a feeling that getting one's way is more important than love because "people don't love me anyhow." "Since no one cares for me, I have to watch out for myself," is an attitude which comes from having been hurt very badly.

We can help ourselves to grow in love if we realize that we don't want to continue in a cycle of lovelessness. If I don't want to be manipulated, shouldn't I, myself, be careful to show respect to others?

Showing respect is a due response of love for another, a person with individual thoughts, feelings, hopes, wounds, longings.

If you happen to be a rather manipulative person, during this next week or two you might look for occasions in which you would ordinarily want to manipulate someone. Then try an honest, respectful approach instead. Record your results in your notebook.

Greed vs. Generosity

A very common vice in our affluent society is acquisitive greed.

Again, you can start your reflections with a narrative of a greedy person's thoughts:

"It seems to me that everything on the earth is meant for our pleasure and that I should have as much of it as I possibly can.

"I love to go to a smorgasbord restaurant or a Sunday brunch where you can eat as much as you want. The first round I eat all the cold things; a huge platter of cucumbers, potato salad, ten olives instead of the one or two usually served at dinners. Then, after finishing all of that, I go back and take some of every single hot dish. In case I get full, I rest awhile, sipping wine or coffee, until I have room for a second of any favorite meat or fish dish. Then I smoke a cigarette and go back for a bit of every dessert. I pile on the whipped cream. It's wonderful.

"No mother or father to force me to stop! I eat as much as I want.

"Sometimes at home in the middle of the night I get up and eat all the goodies in the refrigerator, even though I know my kids will have tantrums when they have no snacks to bring for lunch the next day.

"It's the same when I shop for clothes. I remember when I was a kid I had to take just one of a kind—one pair of jeans, one pair of shoes, one T-shirt. The only things you could get more than one of were underwear and socks—who cares about that? But now I am on my own with a good job and I can just go through the racks and buy anything that catches my eye. What a feeling of luxury not to have to choose between two expensive sweaters—just take out the credit card and buy both! Of course, I sometimes run into a little debt, but I am very generous with my friends and they always help me out with a loan. Sometimes I start getting overweight, or I get too far in debt, and you wouldn't believe how miserable I feel. It's as if my stomach was a bottomless well. I feel such a terrible hunger when I have to eat sparingly. If I can't buy what I like, I become obsessed with the item, daydreaming about it constantly, afraid it will be gone from the store before I can buy it.

"Recently my wife has been pestering me that we should give more money to charity or raise the salaries of the lower echelon workers at my company. That's ridiculous. I've earned the right to have a lot—why give it to strangers?"

Can you add any examples of greed from your own experience or observations of others?

Greed has bad effects on the person with the vice, for usually over-indulgence destroys health and also leads to boredom.

It also hurts others. Here is the way the sight of the greed of others might affect those who have to do without: "I am a poor man. I work as a janitor in a rich neighborhood. Every day on the way to the subway I pass by the fancy restaurants. At my house we eat potatoes every night with some cabbage and soup. We eat meat only once a week. Here at these restaurants I see people drinking wine, having cocktails, eating six courses, sipping after-dinner liqueurs. They give the waiter a tip larger than my daily wage. My boss lives like that, but he won't consider giving me a raise—not on your life!

"Why should they care? They have it made. It's like two different worlds. Sometimes the politicians say that if you vote for them they'll improve the conditions of the poor, but nothing really changes because the rich are never going to vote for anything diminishing their own lifestyle."

Contrast greed with the virtue of generosity:

I know someone who has a very unusual attitude toward possessions. He views everything on earth as belonging first to God and then to God's children in trusteeship. Whatever comes his way is viewed first as a gift and then his, in trust, to use or give away as real needs arise.

He's not miserly. If he thinks that having a very good expensive piano is necessary for the development of his musical gifts, he will buy it; or if he thinks having a nice dessert will lift his spirits at the end of a hard day, he will eat it with gratitude and joy.

But he also can do without. If he is busy helping someone, he could easily skip a meal. He doesn't go around coveting things and longing for them.

He loves to give things away. He gives a tenth of his income to the poor, taking a direct interest in finding causes that are really genuine, and he lends money to people without worrying about it.

Can you add examples?

At first glance, greed can seem very reasonable, even a form of genuine self-love. Why not enjoy the good things of life in abundance?

On the other hand, psychologists and moralists detect other reasons for greed. Some people seem to substitute possessions for love. Some over-react to poverty in childhood by buying more than they will ever use. For some, indulgence and a display of spending power is an attempt to compensate for an inferiority complex.

The philosopher John Stuart Mill once proclaimed it would be better to be a human being dissatisfied than a pig satisfied. Jesus proclaimed: "Man shall not live by bread alone" (Matthew 4:4).

In some very important ways a person who wallows in material goods demeans his or her own personhood. To make the point clearer, try this mental experiment. Suppose you were told you could take a happiness pill guaranteeing pleasant sensations for the rest of your life. The only condition would be that you could make no more choices. You could do nothing. You would just sit in a room by yourself and feel content. How many people do you think would take the pill?

Man is capable of responding to a whole hierarchy of values. There are spiritual values, intellectual values, artistic values, values connected with physical exercise, and values involving enjoyment of sensory things. A person who idol-worships material things out of greed is absolutizing something relative. This impoverishes one's humanity.

What is more, the desire to possess many goods for oneself usually leads indirectly to the impoverishment of the less fortunate. A person who is always over-spending will usually be reluctant to raise the wages of those in his employ. A person who is in debt will naturally vote against bills involving additional taxes, even if this money would be used in programs to help the poor. A person who would be outraged at the idea of a 10% tithe to help the poor, would think nothing of spending 10% of his or her income on luxury items.

On the other hand, good material things do have value. The miserly person is impoverished by stinginess. Tightness of personality prevents a response of gratitude for the good things of the earth and a lack of interest in generous giving to the needy. The generous person places the higher spiritual value of giving above his own enjoyment of material things. He is grateful for all that pleases the senses but he does not idolize them. Hence he is free to receive and to give.

(In a class or group discuss what you think people should contribute in view of the disparity of wealth in our country and in the world. To make it more specific, discuss such issues as the guaranteed income, minimum wage and tax laws. If the discussion seems too general, try this hypothetical experiment: You are a person with an income such that $5,000 a year goes for luxuries. How much of this amount should you give to a cause you are sure will really help the poor with programs of self-development, not just handouts? Aren't you obligated to find such a program? Does a Christian have a special call in this regard?)

After the exercise, write down your conclusion.

Uncontrolled Anger vs. Peacefulness

"It doesn't take much to get me angry. The smallest things can do it a thousand times a day. For example, I'm sitting in the park enjoying the sun, the breeze, the sky. Suddenly it gets a little hotter. I realize I'm going to feel uncomfortable in the sweater I'm wearing. There's no way around it. If I go home and change I'll be annoyed by the inconvenient trip; the mood will be broken. My little paradise is over and I'm churning with anger at the sun...at life!

"Or my car breaks down. Why shouldn't it? I never bother to read the manual or service it. But I get furious at the nerve of the car for failing me. It would feel nice to take a hatchet and break the car into pieces.

"Or I'm reading a novel and have just reached the most exciting part. Just then one of my children comes asking for a peanut-butter sandwich. Fury! How dare he break into the dreamy, romantic oblivion of the novel to demand something so pedestrian as a peanut-butter sandwich? I grind my teeth and put him off. Finally I give in and make him the sandwich. But if he happens to do something a little bad during the next hour, he will really get it!

"You can imagine if this is the way I react when no one is to blame, it's pretty terrible when I have a good reason to be angry!"

(Generally it is agreed that feeling angry at frustrations is perfectly normal and not a vice at all. What makes anger morally evil is when it is out of proportion to the cause or becomes uncontrolled and harmful.) Make a list of situations that make you angry in what you consider to be an uncalled-for degree.

Here is how one of the teenage children of our irate Mom might react:

"Mom is really getting to be a witch.

"Every little thing is like a big crisis. How can her whole face go into a convulsion of anger for such petty reasons? Doesn't she realize how ugly it makes her look?

"Her irritability spoils every situation she is part of. She acts as if everyone were purposely trying to ruin her day—as if life would be paradise except that we are around.

"Most of all, of course, she is the victim—because her life is so disagreeable to her, even though she has so much cause for joy and gratitude."

When you are the victim of irritable angry people, how do you feel? Write it down in your notebook.

Some angry people think that if you don't let out your irritation you will become a repressed individual who someday will break loose and kill someone.

But an alternative to anger is to face annoyances and decide how to handle them successfully.

I know a woman who is a model of peacefulness. Once, when it was clear that we would be late arriving at the airport, we got lost. Instead of becoming frantic, she sat back and resigned herself to the possibility of missing her plane, never losing her peaceful composure.

Coming to see how beautiful and loving a virtue peace can be, is also helpful in developing a less angry way of life.

Sometimes the word "peace" sounds like something nice but unimportant, as compared to dynamic liveliness.

In reality, peace does not mean mediocre compromise and absence of tension, but instead a vibrant, dynamic harmony coming from the flourishing of every being with others according to its own nature. Think of the moments of ecstatic peace in a musical composition, when all the strands of striving, passionate melody join together, leveling off into poignant sweetness. Perhaps we love music so much in our culture because there is so little true harmony anywhere else! An angry person disrupts the natural rhythms of everything around. While one person is dressing in a leisurely way, the angry one is tapping his or her foot, trying to force the other to rush. The shrieks of fighting children or irate parents break into the pleasant hum of everyday activities and shatter everyone's nerves.

Peacefulness, on the contrary, surrounds noise with a blanket of silence until happy sounds re-emerge. The peaceful person lets things be—he or she responds to the goodness of things as they are. The angry person shakes everything up but cannot put humpty dumpty together again after the fit of rage is over.

Lust vs. Purity

"My father is so prudish. He doesn't want me to have any fun. I notice he never kisses my mother or gives her a hug, and they're married! No wonder he's so upset when I get dressed really sexy and go out to a party.

"It's good to be popular. I like to see how it feels to have different guys make love to me. Each one has a slightly special style and it takes away my tensions to get that physical release once a week."

Nowadays many people who are looking for real love have to settle for the warmth of casual encounters. It is said that some couples have sex but don't kiss—that would be too intimate!

A victim of lust may feel cheated: "I thought that girl was truly interested in a meaningful relationship, but after a few dates I saw that she had a roving eye for anyone in pants. It made me feel like a stud."

Lust can seem like a natural response to the sexual attractiveness of others. Why hold back?

On a psychological level, promiscuity seems to manifest a fear of relating in other ways. The lustful person often thinks that she/he has no other reasons for being liked than sex appeal.

Some have been so disappointed in love that they despair of a permanent bond and seek scraps of affection wherever they can find it. Others find they can momentarily overcome feelings of inferiority by the instant popularity which comes with sexual availability.

The virtue of purity comes from a deep response to the worth of the whole person, who deserves to be loved forever in a committed relationship. Sexual intimacy is viewed as a celebration of a love which has reached the point of true self-donation.

Purity is different from prudishness. A prudish person finds the body disgusting and wants to avoid closeness. The pure person desires intimacy but wants it to be real rather than the subtle deception that can exist even in the case of engaged couples who later break up.

Can you relate any stories of people you know who have been victims of lust?

Have you known individuals who love purity but who are not prudish? If so, describe them in your notebook.

There are many other faults which lead to unloving behavior and each one has a corresponding loving virtue.

For example:

Unloving	vs.	Loving
laziness		dedication
prejudice		brotherhood/sisterhood
gossip		understanding silence
phoniness		sincerity
harshness		mercy
conceit		humility
envy		contentment
ingratitude		gratitude

Can you add any to this list?

Your Program for Personal Moral Growth

Most people wish that they could diminish suffering and add to the joy of the world. Very often it is because of our chief vice that we victimize others. Just because this is so ingrained in our character, we tend to give up on changing and just hope that people will forgive us. If people are very good, they probably will. But why not show our love by making an effort to change?

What do you think is one of your worst vices at the present time? (You need not choose the one that would be most embarrassing to write about.) In your notebook write the name of the fault you have in mind. If you don't think you have any, write down conceit!

What virtue is the opposite of your fault? If you are not sure, consult others.

If you are not sure of your vice, ask your friends and relatives. In most cases they will all come up with the same one!

Now write a narrative in your notebook describing some typical scenes in which you exhibit your vice:

Describe the miseries of your victims. (In some cases, such as sloppiness, you may be the victim!)

Next, imagine yourself exhibiting the opposite virtue in a few typical situations. Write your descriptions.

Can you explain the motives and psychological causes of why you fall into this vice?

Explain why the virtue opposed to your fault can be a way of being more loving toward others.

Now write down some of your favorite excuses for your fault.

To keep a journal of your moral growth in love regarding this vice and its virtue, carry a large piece of paper in your pocket. For two weeks make notes about situations in which you fell into your vice or exhibited the virtue. Note also your own reactions to others who victimize you by the same fault or who gratify you by the opposite virtue.

At the end of your account, write out a plan for continuing your path of love.

In a group you might share incidents and resolutions.

Obviously, the same method could be used to make progress over your other faults.

More will be written about faults and virtues in the sections on the relationship of God to living a life of love.

Steps in Making Loving Decisions

As well as developing a personality full of loving rather than unloving qualities, it is also very important to avoid making unloving decisions and to make loving ones.

The series of steps suggested here is not definitive. As will be explained in the section on the religious dimension of love, many will decide that without God's help they are not strong enough to opt for the good of others if the sacrifice is too extreme.

However, I believe it is important to see what steps toward making loving decisions could be taken by anyone, religious or not.

These are the steps in making loving decisions that will be dealt with in the rest of this chapter:

1. recommitting yourself to a personal philosophy of love
2. avoiding self-centered excuses

3. finding out what is truly loving and unloving

4. integrating loving choices into your lifestyle.

For purposes of illustration, I will be using a particular ethical decision as an example.

Lisa has been going out with Mark ever since they both started at St. Mary's college. They are very close. Both of them want to become doctors. They decided that they didn't want to have to make a choice between each other and their careers, but instead would wait for marriage until they both finished medical school. Their parents are helping to pay their bills for room and board, but they are both on scholarship for the tuition.

In their junior year, they decided it was old-fashioned to wait for marriage in order to express their love for each other physically in the most complete way. Lisa, a biology major familiar with her own bodily rhythms, had a pretty good idea as to when the fertile time of her cycle was, so they just avoided intercourse on those days. But one night when they had been to a party, both of them were very high and went ahead, even though it was a borderline day in the cycle.

Lisa is pregnant. She is trying to decide what to do. Should she drop out of school, arrange a quick marriage, have the baby, and postpone her own plans for a career for many years while she brings up their child? Or wouldn't it be so much easier to call it a mistake, have a fast abortion, and be more careful in the future?

In this section, I am going to have Lisa decide for an abortion. In her deliberations, she will use such concepts as these:

"It's really for the greatest good of all concerned."

"The fetus is too small to suffer."

"Nowadays people realize that a woman's career counts too; she's not just a baby machine."

"Everybody's doing it."

At this point I will *presuppose* that Lisa and Mark agree that a fetus is human. Later I will explain why this is true.

Farther on (in Step III), I will have Lisa and Mark decide that abortion is an unloving act and that they will keep their baby.

As you study the decision-making steps in this chapter, you may choose a decision you have to make now or can imagine yourself making in the future. In your notebook write a brief description of the matter you will consider. When further on I will refer to "your own ethical decision," you should respond in terms of the problem you now select.

Step I
Recommitment to a
Personal Philosophy of Love

In a moment of indecision we often feel pulled back and forth by the pleasant or unpleasant consequences we foresee on each side.

In making a loving decision, it is important to step back for a moment and recommit ourselves to choosing for love regardless of the cost to ourselves. This does not always mean choosing what will hurt us most. Often what is good for us is also good for others. It does mean not clinging to our own will regardless of the harm to those affected.

In the case of Lisa and Mark, the pre-med college students, I am supposing that their first reaction to the knowledge of the unwanted pregnancy was panic.

Lisa started thinking of women she had known, including her own mother, who had married early in similar circumstances. "I don't want to wind up like her." Mark pictured dropping out of school, living in a trailer and working at the supermarket.

They did not stop to consider their deeper mutual wish to be a force for good in the world, starting with each other and their own family.

In the case of your own ethical decision—the one you have selected to reflect upon—before considering consequences, first of all commit yourself to love, in terms of your own personal way of viewing love in life.

Step II
Avoiding Self-Centered Excuses

In Lisa's panic certain phrases came immediately into her mind: "I've gotta survive; nobody's going to be hurt if I have an early abortion."

Mark thought, "We'll feel guilty the day of the abortion but later we'll be glad. Our consciences won't bother us because what we're doing is for the greatest good of all concerned. Unwanted babies are unhappy. We can have as many as we want later on. Think of the good Lisa and I will do in our medical work!"

Just before the abortion Lisa began to feel guilty. It seemed terribly wrong to snuff out the life of a tiny human being. Then she thought, "It *is* wrong, but nobody's perfect. I'm not a saint. God will forgive me."

Some of you might think the reasoning used by Lisa and Mark is justified. I think that even though they were trying to be good, they were using self-centered excuses.

Here are some ways that the phrases Lisa and Mark used can be shown to spring often from selfishness rather than love.

"I Gotta Survive."

It was on a university campus during the '70's that I first started to hear the phrase, "I've got to survive," used as a self-evident maxim.

It puzzled me. Naturally I had read of cases in wartime or in totalitarian countries or in the history of the martyrs where people were given an immediate choice:

"Do what we say or die." And there were also sudden emergencies when trying to save someone else might mean risking one's own life.

Even though we laud heroes and heroines for choosing death over survival, we could understand if someone would refuse, saying: "My survival counts too." In such situations the concept of survival seems like one of many good motivations—not a phony excuse.

But in the contemporary use of the concept of survival, there is usually no question whatsoever of so radical a choice. To have a right to survive seems to mean simply that nothing should be allowed to stand in the way of what I conceive to be my own fulfillment.

At the foundation of *survival* as an excuse, we can find the very old philosophy of egocentric hedonism.

In Runes' *Dictionary of Philosophy* hedonism is defined: "A doctrine as to what entities possess intrinsic value. According to it, pleasure and this alone has positive value, is intrinsically good...the contrary hedonic feeling tone is displeasure...and this alone has negative ultimate value...the total value of an action is the net intrinsic value of all its hedonic consequences."

In simpler language, when a hedonist is egocentric, he or she will maintain that it is perfectly all right to seek the greatest possible pleasure for oneself, wherever that may lie, no matter how many victims.

There are different kinds of pleasures. The most obvious are the sensory delights associated with eating, sleeping, sexuality, sun-bathing, etc. But some people are ready to give up many of these sensual pleasures for more complicated ones such as the excitement of power, or pride in climbing one rung after another of the ladder of success.

For some of us the word hedonist sounds ugly. We would not apply it to ourselves with gleeful bravado. However, if we have the courage to check on ourselves, we may detect such a philosophy behind the most ordinary perceptions. For example, when we say, "I had a good day," we usually mean that many pleasurable things happened—i.e., I had a nice lunch, someone praised me or I won out over my chief enemy at work. By a "good day" we rarely mean a day devoted to the welfare of others amidst many frustrations. Such a day we more aptly describe with the negative: "My whole day was shot!" A "lousy day" is often one without pleasure because we were forced to be helpful to others!

Many factors go into making a decision, but for the sake of philosophical clarity, let's isolate the hedonistic elements in the decision of Lisa and Mark.

Aborting their baby has lots of pluses for this couple. It means they can enjoy the freedom to pursue their careers without obstacles. It means they don't have to contemplate the ills of living poorly at the start of their marriage. They don't have to worry about getting into a "forced marriage" they may later regret.

Of course there is the pain of guilt and a fear of possible bad physical consequences of abortion. They may have to cope with disapproval if their parents find out.

But balancing things out, the pleasures seem to far outweigh the pains. This is not the only reason Lisa and Mark decided for the abortion but it is probably a large factor, for it is only human nature to want to choose what seems most desirable in terms of our own individual needs.

Now consider the ethical issue you are debating in your own life. Could the pleasures and displeasures over-weigh in your mind the question as to which decision would be most loving?

Write your tentative answer in your notebook.

But, you may ask, why is hedonism unloving or wrong? Isn't it loving to want to maximize pleasure and minimize displeasure?

Here are some problems concerning hedonism for you to consider.

First of all, our decisions often have unwanted consequences. We simply do not know the future well enough to predict what is for the greater good.

In later life Lisa may discover (and this would not be unusual) that because of the first abortion she will have a real difficulty in carrying a baby to term. After many miscarriages she may deeply regret her college decision. Also, her boyfriend may have pretended to go along with that decision but might not respect her as highly as before.

Lisa may not find her medical career as thrilling as she imagined and may wish she had not sacrificed her baby for it.

Plunging into their studies, Mark and Lisa may have less and less time for each other. Their ideal match may never work out.

The drive to succeed, which led them to decide to sacrifice their baby, may also lead them to lose their love for the value of life, so that their humanitarian motives for being doctors may fade, leaving them with a sense of emptiness.

The sense of guilt may grow rather than diminish. Some women who once opted for abortion can't look at a baby on the street without feeling a wrench of pain. Some have nightmares all their lives.

In the case of your own ethical decision, can you think of any unwanted consequences that could occur if you make a selfish choice?

"My Conscience Doesn't Bother Me."

"I feel good about it. My conscience doesn't bother me!" This is probably one of the most frequently heard excuses for moral evil.

Of course, as we shall see later on, there can be a legitimate conscience claim in a choice that runs counter to the usual pattern of a society. We can all think of heroes who after long introspection made brave decisions that shocked persons who were blind to some particular moral value. Socrates was tried for impiety; Jesus, for blasphemy. Gandhi and Martin Luther King were subjected to ridicule for their non-violence. In these cases great sacrifices, even to death, were necessary in the following of conscience.

Recently, however, it seems that the word *conscience* has been most often used not for making hard decisions that demand sacrifice but for rationalizing refusal to accept the sacrifices demanded by morality. "Conscience" always seems to instruct us that we don't have to overcome temptations or endure hardships.

Notice that Lisa and Mark tried to make a decision in conscience, but that the decision also turned out to be what each favored for his or her own reasons.

One problem which enables persons to make unloving decisions "in good conscience" is value-blindness.

In his book *Ethics*, Von Hildebrand develops the penetrating concept of value-blindness in order to explain why there can be so much divergence among people's ideas of right and wrong.[1]

Just as some people may be blind to certain colors, human beings can also be blind with regard to particular objective moral values. Examples that readers would certainly agree with would include the blindness of the Nazis to the worth of the Jewish people or the blindness of some Americans of the past and even of our own times to the dignity of the Black race.

A fascinating commentary on value-blindness can be found in this comparison chart that recently appeared in a newspaper:

---

1. Dietrich Von Hildebrand, *Ethics* (Chicago: Franciscan Herald Press, 1953), pp. 46ff.

Another "Civil War" that <u>Must</u> Be Won —If the U.S. Is to Survive!

1857 'DRED SCOTT' ABORTION DECISION 1973 !

- IN THE INFAMOUS "DRED SCOTT" SUPREME COURT DECISION OF 1857, THE "BLACK SLAVE" WAS LABELED AS JUST "A PIECE OF PROPERTY" OF THE <u>WHITE MAN.</u>

- IN THE EQUALLY NOTORIOUS RULING BY OUR PRESENT SUPREME COURT, THE "INNOCENT CHILD" IS NOW DISMISSED AS JUST ANOTHER DEPENDENT "SLAVE" BELONGING TO A <u>WOMAN</u>...TO DISPOSE OF AS SHE SEES FIT!

Thus:

Slavery–1857	Abortion–1973
Although he may have a heart and a brain, and he may be a human life biologically, a slave is not a legal person. The Dred Scott decision by the United States Supreme Court has that clear.	Although he may have a heart and a brain, and he may be a human life biologically, an unborn baby is not a legal person. Our courts have now made that clear!
A Black man only becomes a legal person when he is set free. Before that time, we should not concern ourselves about him because he has no legal rights.	A baby only becomes a legal person when he is born. Before that time, we should not concern ourselves about him because he has no legal rights.
If you think that slavery is wrong, then nobody is forcing you to be a slave-owner. But don't impose your morality on somebody else!	If you think abortion is wrong, then nobody is forcing you to have one. But don't impose your morality on somebody else!
A man has a right to do what he wants with his own property.	A woman has a right to do what she wants with her own body.
Isn't slavery really something merciful? After all, every Black man has a right to be protected. Isn't it better never to be set free than to be sent unprepared, and ill-equipped, into a cruel world? (Spoken by someone already free!)	Isn't abortion really something merciful? After all, every baby has a right to be wanted. Isn't it better never to be born than to be sent alone and unloved into a cruel world? (Spoken by someone already born!)

Some value-blindness comes to us as a cultural heritage. In certain countries polygamy has been practiced for so long that almost everyone is blind to the higher value of monogamy. Such value-blindness, according to Von Hildebrand, is relatively blameless, although in the case of many participants the custom is adhered to partly because it satisfies a vice common to people of all countries, such as lust.

But other types of value-blindness come because we allow our desires to overcome our original moral feelings, principles or religious convictions. For example, Lisa's frantic fear of seeing her career dreams go down the drain may temporarily blind her to the great objective value of the life within her womb.

If you can, describe value-blindness as it might function with regard to your own moral issue. Write the description in your notebook.

One-sided sympathies can be another cause of blindness. Persons close to someone who has to make an ethical decision may be accused of a special sort of blindness, due to one-sided sympathies which lead to a sincere but erroneous conscience.

Let us think of Lisa's example. Suppose she turns to her father for advice. The father is probably very sympathetic to his daughter's plight. He may resent the boyfriend and rage against the stupidity of the young man in being so careless. The question of the baby's right to life may scarcely cross his mind. After all, his daughter who cries hysterically in her bedroom looks like the main victim, whereas the baby has no voice.

Since Lisa's father has a good motive in wanting to protect his daughter, he may have a clear conscience about recommending abortion.

False liberation is another reason why peoples' consciences may not bother them even if their decision is unloving.

Many people feel positively liberated when they plunge into what they previously knew to be evil. Why is that?

For one thing, after the long, hard struggle of a difficult decision, it is a relief to decide either way. Then again, most of us hate to feel constrained from doing what seems most pleasurable or advantageous to ourselves. As a passionate desire overwhelms us, the principles we live by begin to seem very cold and remote—not really powerful enough to win the battle. It is a good feeling to be done with them and to swing totally into the rhythm of our desires. We feel triumphant when we can overcome all scruples and do what we want to do. Only later may we come to see that evil did not really liberate us. Meanwhile, we may feel very happy and readily convince ourselves that our decision cannot be so wrong.

Lisa has a very strong desire to keep up with the timetable she set for her advancement from college to medical school. She doesn't want to have a baby right now. In the face of her thwarted ambitions, the ethical principle that life is sacred seems a distant ideal rather than a burning reality. Compared to the nightmare of years of being stuck with diapers and housework while her husband flies along ahead of her at medical school, the idea of abortion provides a false sense of liberation.

Even though conscience can be used as an excuse for unloving behavior, many consider it our best source for making decisions.

Situation Ethics is the name of the theory which states that we should try to discover what is right to do by examining each unique situation and listening to our consciences instead of following a set of ethical rules.

In defense of conscience, the situation ethicist will claim that it is impossible to just walk through life with a rule book. That would be tunnel vision. We must make our own judgments, for it is the glory of being free human beings that we can decide for ourselves.

If we have good motives, wanting to do the most loving thing in every situation, why should we doubt that we will accomplish more good than evil by relying on the judgment of conscience?

The situation ethicist declares that even should one's conscience be erroneous at times, it is still better to decide for oneself than to let others make the decision.

In response, I would agree that in many situations the consciences of good persons will warn them away from objective evil and show them the good. However, I would disagree with the situation ethicist on the whole, because I think that more often than not, especially in situations involving crisis and sacrifice, conscience does not function as a register of the objective good but instead conforms with principles which are questionable.

The situation ethicist pictures conscience as a light shining in the darkness, whereas I picture conscience as a very complex product of early training, fear of punishment, need for approval, false principles—not always a pure response to what is objectively good and evil.

Because of the ambiguity in the way conscience functions, I cannot regard it as a self-evident proof of ethical goodness if I feel good about something and my conscience doesn't bother me.

We must draw our moral convictions from a source other than our own subjective judgments in each situation. Having established a set of objective values, as we will attempt to do in Step III, we will be able to form our conscience by these, so that it can warn us of violations in the disturbing, tempting situations in which we find ourselves.

"It's for the Greater Good. Nobody Will Be Hurt."

Lisa and Mark may object that they are not hedonists but humanitarians. They *really* think the abortion is for the greater good because nobody will be hurt.

Many people base the lovingness or unlovingness of a choice on whether anyone is being hurt. For example, in a secret adultery the unfaithful husband or wife often claims that since the spouse doesn't know, it's okay; it may even hold the marriage together if the unhappy partner has some joy elsewhere.

One of the problems with this excuse is that not all victims scream. The rejected spouse may know all along and feel very hurt but be afraid to complain for fear of losing the adulterous spouse altogether.

Lisa may try to picture the fetus as a clump of cells rather than a tiny baby able to suffer pain. With regard to the sentiments of her boyfriend, who may have secretly wished she had kept the baby, she will erase the memory of his hurt and shock from her mind by thinking of his eventual relief at a decision involving less sacrifice for him. If her parents are very upset about the decision, she will decide that they have no right to feel bad since it is none of their business. In this way she will build up her defenses against any hurt she has caused, until she may really think that her act has been without victims.

The fetus didn't scream aloud so it doesn't seem to have been maltreated, although evidence now shows the baby in the womb does try to scream as its limbs are dismembered.

Besides quiet victims there can be long-term victims. Lisa's decision may influence other friends to take the same course of action, increasing the number of victims in the world. Her boyfriend, Mark, may find himself adopting a previously unwelcome pro-abortion position as a way of defending himself against guilt feelings. This pro-abortion stance may influence his friends and his own practice of medicine in years to come.

Can you think of any possible quiet or long-term victims in the case of the ethical choice you yourself must confront?

Even when one sincerely wants to find out what is for the greatest good, it is very difficult to know. This has been one of the chief criticisms of the theory of utilitarianism.

Utilitarianism is defined in Runes' *Dictionary of Philosophy* as "the view that the right act is the act which, of all those open to the agent, will actually or probably produce the greatest amount of pleasure or happiness in the world at large."

The greatest advocate of this theory was John Stuart Mill (1806-1873), a prominent liberal reformer of his day. Oppressed by the visible suffering of the poor and the violation of the natural rights of women, he sought to replace moral ideas based on tradition with a more open ethical system based on evidence and concern for consequences.

By means of the utilitarian formula—act to produce the greatest good for the greatest number—Mill sought to overcome that selfishness which tends to count the self alone as important and others as zero. Since you, yourself, would only count for one in any utilitarian survey, you would be bound to see the necessity of sacrificing your own claims in the face of the needs of so many others. Mill believed that through education mankind would gradually learn to realize that one's personal greatest good is whatever is the greatest good for the whole.

Although Mill himself never drew from his theory the consequence that the end would justify the means, according to many critics this seems to follow without fail, both philosophically and historically. Given grave enough concern for particular goods for a large number of people, will not any means seem justified? Historically, have not totalitarian regimes insisted that the progress of all humanity in ages to come justified the death here and now of a few thousand or even of millions?

As mentioned earlier in connection with the excuse "nobody's suffering," it is not easy to predict accurately how many victims will result from a particular action.

Mill was himself inclined to think that there were certain rules which would always bring about the greatest good for the greatest number. Murder, for example, would always be judged to lead to further bad consequences for mankind at large in terms of creating a general climate of fear and defensiveness, even if in the short run it might seem justifiable.

However, utilitarian philosophy led to other world-wide consequences that Mill did not predict.

Freed from the idea that some deeds such as murder were always wrong (and therefore, of course, unloving), many leaders in such movements as Nazism and Communism justified mass genocide. Later, some such leaders repented of their false calculation, for the result of their acts was not heaven but hell.

In regard to abortion, Bernard Nathanson, a doctor who spearheaded liberal abortion laws and ran a huge abortion clinic, finally saw that the fetus is human. Dr. Nathanson now exhausts himself trying to undo the laws he initiated. Many observers see lack of accountability of fathers, infanticide of the disabled, acceptance of euthanasia, and forced sterilization all as a domino effect from abortion.

"Everybody's Doing It."

Still, to many it seems impossible that anything can be too unloving if "everybody's" doing it, even some otherwise loving people.

This excuse takes many forms. I see it hidden behind such statements as these:

1. "That opinion went out with the Middle Ages. Boy, are you old-fashioned!"

2. "Even person X thinks it's okay, so how could it be wrong?"

3. "Statistics show...."

4. "The laws of the land allow it."

Of course, it could sometimes happen that the majority view, or the latest view, or the one held by an admired person or the one just voted in, would really be the right view. But, as I will try to show later, it seems to me that a view is not made true because many people hold it, or because the best people believe it, or even because it is the newest view. An opinion is true if it corresponds to what is really right. More of this in a later chapter; for now, let us examine "majority wins" exclusively as it functions in rationalizing a wrong act.

Lisa certainly feels less guilty about her abortion when she hears of lots of other college girls doing it. When the act was illegal she would have hesitated much more, not only because of risks to her health, but because of reluctance to move out of the stream of what decent citizens thought was right. The idea that the Supreme Court of the land, so respected by most Americans, has left it up to her and her doctor is reassuring. The connection of the word "liberal" with abortion adds a sheen of progress to the idea, for it links "anti-abortion" with forces of regression.

How does this excuse apply to one side or another of your own ethical dilemma?

Sociologists have popularized the very apt term "peer pressure," showing the impact of this force on the individual. We all greatly need to be accepted by the people around us. Thinking, speaking or acting contrary to the majority view of our group is experienced as very painful and disconcerting, and only the brave few can withstand such a force toward conformity.

But we also know from history that every era has its particular blind spots. The marvelously intellectual and artistic Greeks were blind to the evil of slavery. There were times in gentlemanly England when it was thought harmless to base the economy on the labor of young children. Some societies tolerated infant sacrifice in religious rites. Millions of Germans considered Hitler a tremendous force for progress. This shows that even the most admired leaders can be insane tyrants, hardly to be followed with blind trust.

History also shows that there are cycles of decay within whole societies where what once would have been considered repugnant and criminal becomes an accepted lifestyle.

For the same reasons, the fact that hardly anyone considers abortion very wrong anymore is a weak argument. The legalizing of abortion could be a sign that our society is decaying.

The abolitionists certainly thought that the legalization of slavery was a terrible infringement on the original spirit of the Declaration of Independence. The fact that most people accepted it as a necessary evil in no way convinced them that this practice could be tolerated. *How would this critique apply to the moral problem you are working on?*

"Nobody's Perfect; I'm Not a Saint."

What about the final excuse Lisa gives: "I know it's wrong, but I'm not a saint"?

Here again we find ourselves with a statement that sounds almost self-evident and yet can be used in very phony ways as an excuse.

Everyone knows that human beings are not perfect and that very few are saints. It can seem harsh to demand so much authenticity of Lisa and Mark. But even so, it hardly seems right that a person who is victimizing you should demand that you exonerate him or her on that basis. Suppose a thief were in the act of stealing your car, and you yelled at him to stop and he said, "I'm not perfect and neither are you—what do you expect?" Not only would you refuse to buy this excuse, but you would consider him to be adding insult to injury!

If you were Lisa's baby and could speak, wouldn't you want a chance to live even if Lisa and Mark were not perfect? After all, our own real-life parents were not perfect, yet we are glad they were good enough to have given us life.

It seems to me that the phrase "nobody's perfect" is extremely interesting to analyze.

In the mouth of someone consoling a guilt-stricken person who is unable to forgive himself or herself for some past deed, the words "nobody's perfect; you're not a saint" could be very meaningful and helpful. And yet, in the mouth of someone excusing himself from a moral obligation, the words are full of unjustifiable anger, pride and insulting bravado.

When used as an excuse, "Nobody's perfect" seems to throw the blame on the ideal in question instead of on the guilty party. It is as if God, society, parents or friends, in holding up an ideal of motherly protectiveness of the young, had proposed something impossible for the sole purpose of making others feel guilty.

But surely any system of ethics, whether religious or humanistic, must be based on some ideal which over-reaches man's natural tendencies to selfishness, especially as these gain ascendance in moments of crisis! There could be no society at all if everyone simply felt free to trample on everyone else, totally giving in to the lowest instincts of one's nature without a struggle.

We should forgive and yet also inspire others to be better.

Referring to the ethical situation you are studying, what effect would you predict if all ideals were taken out of the picture?

Step III
Finding Out
What Is Truly Loving and Unloving

In this section, I will try to show how Lisa and Mark become more loving by deciding to keep their baby.

I will suppose that, after the shock of finding out that Lisa is pregnant, all the excuses described in Step II pass through their heads—but that finally they agree that these could be just selfish excuses, and so they sit down to deliberate about what would really be the right—i.e., the most loving—course of action.

It happens that Lisa and Mark are both taking ethics at this time. The professor brings in a film about abortion. When it shows how abortion works by methods which dismember the fetus, vacuum it out, burn it to death with saline solution, or kill it by other methods equally horrifying, Lisa and Mark "just know" that such an act could not be an act of love for a baby.

A more formal name for "just knowing that something is right or wrong" is ethical intuition.

The use of the word "intuition" here is a precise philosophical one. It does not mean an irrational hunch but rather an immediate intellectual apprehension.

An ethical intuitionist is one who believes that we know the goodness of the good and the worth of various values by an immediate apprehension rather than by deduction of consequences.

For example, once you have experienced a genuinely reverent person, you can easily see that, in terms of goodness, reverence is preferable to manipulation. As long as you compare manipulation to the pseudo-virtue of passivity, you may think that manipulation is not so bad, but when you have an intuitive intellectual grasp of the essence of reverence as a moral quality, you cannot help but perceive its goodness.

Exponents of ethical intuitionism are such philosophers as G. E. Moore, Max Scheler and Dietrich Von Hildebrand.

The key objects of ethical intuitionism are the *good, quality,* (in the sense in which Pirsig uses it in his popular *Zen and the Art of Motorcycle Maintenance),* and *value.*

Of the *good,* the contemporary British intuitionist Iris Murdoch states that no realist can deny that goodness really matters. We can pretend that egoism is justified, but we all know that ruthless stampeding over the rights of others is wrong.

In the philosophy of the Catholic moral philosopher Dietrich Von Hildebrand, *value* is viewed as a type of importance. *Good* is the property of a being which enables it to motivate our will or to engender an affective response in us because of its positive importance. A value is something intrinsically important. We recognize that whether we get a lollipop or not is of no intrinsic importance, but whether we act justly or unjustly does matter very much.

Discussion of value theory is rather confusing to most modern people, because the word "value" is used in at least two very different ways, not only in ordinary language but also in philosophy and education.

Value theory springing out of the pragmatic school of thought makes it seem as if there is no intrinsic value in an object—instead, we decide to give something value in accordance with our own personal taste. For example, in a book called *Values and Teaching* by Raths, Harmin and Simon, we find references which describe values as individual, created by us, changing, never to be indoctrinated. The function of man is not to watch over ancient values, but to enjoy the excitement of forming his or her own lifestyle.

In a market economy it is natural for us to think of economic values as the paradigm—and such values go up and down with the stock exchange.

Such a meaning of value in which nothing is fixed and we create values ourselves, is exactly opposite to the notion of values in the European phenomenological school, in which we *discover* rather than *create* values. Values are seen as eternally valid, as transcending relativism. The noble deed of a Roman senator has a value which can be perceived by a reader in the 20th century. Risking one's life to save someone else is always the embodiment of high value. To be kind rather than cruel must be understood as good in itself. If in a particular culture cruelty is exalted, this is described by thinkers such as Von Hildebrand as a form of value-blindness.

Of course, some object: How can you know if anything is really absolutely good or evil—since philosophers disagree, and so do whole societies?

This difficulty will be met later on. For now, suppose that there are some intrinsic values, and let's see how these values can be divided to help us to understand the intuitive knowledge that Lisa and Mark reached regarding their decision.

Von Hildebrand has provided us with some very helpful categories for the analysis of conflict and value-blindness. In his book, *Ethics* (Franciscan Herald Press), he distinguishes between what he calls *the subjectively satisfying* (what gives us personal pleasure regardless of its objective goodness, such as smoking, a particular flavor of ice cream, etc.); *the objective good for the person* (what is truly of benefit to the human being, though changing, such as education, dishwashers, cars); and *unchanging intrinsic values* (what is precious in itself in time and eternity, such as beauty, truth, peace, the unique selfhood of a human person, God).

In many cases of moral choice we find a conflict between these three categories—the subjectively satisfying, the objective good for the person and the intrinsic value. For example, we find Macbeth contemplating the murder of the king, perfectly aware that *loyalty* to his king, a man of high moral character, is an *intrinsic value*, and that *hospitality* is an *objective good* which he owes to the king. Yet, on the other side, there is Macbeth's passionate ambition for the *subjective* satisfaction of his pride: he wants to be king himself. As the witches prophesy his ascent to the throne, and his wife urges him to the terrible deed of murder, the longing for the subjective satisfaction of being king overwhelms him, temporarily blinding him to the intrinsic evil of the deed.

In the case of Kitty Genovese—a woman raped and murdered in front of an apartment development while thirty-eight people watched from their windows and did nothing, in order to avoid getting involved—we have an example of temporary blindness to the intrinsic evil of failing to help a neighbor. This blindness stemmed from fear of the subjectively dissatisfying annoyances connected with calling the police and being interrogated.

In the case of the decision of Lisa and Mark, here is a list of elements in conflict:

Subjective pleasures or displeasures

anticipated joy of fondling the baby
or disgust with drooling, diaper-using babies
fun of being free
fun of being unencumbered
displeasure from morning sickness, fatigue, labor pains
displeasure of males at one's pregnant image
displeasure from ridicule for being unwed mother
pleasure of parental approval
or displeasure of parental anger

Objective goods at stake

baby—the good this child can experience and bring to others
health of mother—damaged by pregnancy or abortion
psychological health of mother and father—threatened by pregnancy and abortion
smooth continuation of career without interruption
not being forced into early marriage which might not work
finance—strained by having a baby
quality of life of baby

Eternal values

unique personality of baby
unending bond of love between mother, father and child (in potency)

A pro-life proponent would insist that those who approve of abortions have simply become blind to the eternal values at stake because of concern for a category of lesser importance—objective goods or subjective pleasures. To the pro-lifer, the unique personality of the baby is the highest value on the human level, and no other consideration can be higher.

A *defender* of the abortion option would claim that there is no eternal value at stake. This person's highest value would be one of the items listed under "objective goods" or rarely, but conceivably, one of those listed under "subjective pleasures." With eyes fixed on some objective good, such as the psychological health of the mother or the anticipated quality of life of the infant, a pro-abortionist would think that he or she was doing something good in helping a young woman to decide for an abortion.

It should be noted that the option of giving the child over for *adoption* preserves the unique value of the baby while avoiding many of the subjective displeasures and objective sacrifices.

Now turn to the ethical issue that you are working on and list the subjectively satisfying pleasures, objective goods and eternal values involved.

(In a group you may want to discuss your answers to help each other.)

Although ethical intuitionism can trace its roots as far back as Plato and Augustine, it has only become prominent as an explicit theory of ethical knowledge in the 20th century.

A more traditional Christian ethical philosophy which shows that some acts are objectively evil, and therefore clearly also unloving, is the philosophy of *natural law.*

The philosopher Germain Grisez gives a very clear explanation of this theory. According to Grisez, moral goodness and badness can be discerned by comparing the essential patterns of possible human actions with the intelligible structure of human nature considered both in its inner complexity and in its intrinsic relationships.[2]

When we examine human nature we discover, as did Thomas Aquinas, that all men seek: life and its preserva-

---

2. Germain Grisez, *Contraception and Natural Law* (Milwaukee: Bruce, 1964).

tion, sex, care of offspring, etc. By virtue of our rational faculties, we seek truth, life in society, etc. For example, according to Thomas Aquinas lying is evil in itself. Since words are naturally the signs of what is understood, it is unnatural for a person to signify by word what he does not have in his mind. A lie has the character of a sin not only because of the damage that is done to a neighbor, but in its own disorder.

By means of practical reason we apply the natural law to the ordering of our lives, seeking principles about objectives. The first principle of natural law according to St. Thomas Aquinas is: "The good is that which all things seek after. Good is to be done and promoted and evil is to be avoided."

Relating the needs of human nature and the overall principles enunciated above, you can come up with such clear concepts as: Life is a good and actions which preserve it are good, whereas actions opposed to life should be avoided. Good food preserves life and is to be preferred to poison.

Since the basic needs of mankind are deemed by natural-law theorists to be self-evident, it is wrong to take action against any one of them in order to maximize another, for example, to improve society by getting rid of half its members.

It is the work of ethical philosophers and social and political theorists to work out the basic principles of natural law to be applied to the issues which arise in our changing historical situations. The meaning of a universal rule is very carefully defined through reasoning.

For example, most natural-law theorists would not make a blanket statement such as "do not kill" without first defining the difference between murder, self-defense, etc. Natural-law theory, while aiming at universality so that an individual does not selfishly exclude himself, is not simplistic in its pronouncements, because the rules include the necessary specifications, such as self-defense.

In order to relate natural-law theory to a topic such as abortion, it is first necessary to define terms in view of the best available estimate of the facts. Taking it as self-evident that it is morally wrong to destroy the life of a human being except in self-defense, it is necessary to determine whether in fact the organism within the mother's womb is a human being.

Being pre-med students, Lisa and Mark are especially interested in the following facts when trying to decide about their own problem.

Here is a summary of the biological traits of the unborn baby at different points in time.

conception	—	the fertilized ovum has its own unique genetic code with human cells.
3-4 weeks	—	eyes, spinal cord, brain, thyroid gland, lungs, stomach, liver, kidneys, intestines. Heart begins beating between the 18th and 25th days.
4 weeks	—	head is taking definite shape; arms and legs forming.
5 weeks	—	1/3" tall. Eyes have retina and lens; ear clefts; arms and legs are developing with fingers and toes.
6½ weeks	—	fetus floats in amniotic sack. Facial features visible; mouth and tongue formed; 20 baby teeth forming in gums; major muscle system developed.
8 weeks	—	eyes complete; mouth has lips; fingers and toes complete; swims in surrounding fluid. Brain is complete; brain waves measurable on EEG. Baby is capable of feeling pain. MOST DECISIONS FOR ABORTION MADE AT THIS TIME.
12 weeks	—	3½" tall. Swallows regularly; vocal chords complete; cries silently; fingernails appear; may start sucking thumb.
16 weeks	—	5½" tall; weight 6 oz. Eyebrows and lashes appear; grasps with hands; swims; kicks; somersaults.
20 weeks	—	has a chance of survival as premature infant outside the womb.

The facts clearly indicate that the unborn entity in the mother's womb is certainly not a mere blob of cells. A mother who decides for abortion on the basis of such a conception is basing her choice on false data.

On the other hand, the question which many raise is whether the human *life* in the womb is to be considered a human *person* in the full sense of the word.

Most pro-lifers reason that any designation except personhood at conception makes no sense. It is at conception that the genes of a human, rather than those of a cat, join together. It is the very nature of human selfhood to begin small and develop. No one stage of development can be decisive—only the beginning. As the philosopher James Hanink expresses it: "Every identifiable and existing adult human being has once been a fetus—though never just a sperm or an ovum. But unless some adult human beings have a history of past membership in other species, or in none, no existing adult has ever not been a member of homosapiens. So fetuses are human beings."[3]

It is further argued by such natural-law theorists as Fr. Robert Taylor, S.J., of Loyola Marymount University, that properties of humanity such as consciousness, intelligence, free will, etc. are manifestations of the more fundamental reality of being a subject. The unconditional value of the human being is grounded in being an individual subject. This value does not disappear when the subject fails to manifest a certain potentiality, as in the case of a fetus, a person in a coma, etc.

If we think of natural law in terms of theology as well as philosophy, we can see that each individual is infinitely precious as one loved into being by God, the Father of all being.[4]

---

3. James Hanink, "Persons, Rights and the Problem of Abortion," Ph.D. Thesis, Michigan State University, 1975.

4. See Dietrich Bonhoeffer, *Ethics*, (New York: The Macmillan Co., 1955), pp. 149ff.

Do you think there are any natural rights pertaining to the very nature of the human person in society which are at stake in your own ethical issue? List them in your notebook.

Lisa and Mark decide to discuss their decision with their ethics professor. Later, when the excuses will begin to seem attractive, they will be helped in overcoming temptation by remembering a one-line injunction that their teacher told them had first been enunciated by the philosopher Immanuel Kant (1724-1804):

"There is but one categorical imperative: act only on that maxim whereby thou canst at the same time will that it should become a universal law."

Let us try to explain it in simple terms.

You are about to do something—say, tell a lie. Before making the decision to go ahead, ask yourself this question: "What would happen if everyone told lies?" You will discover that you could never will the universal maxim, "Everyone should tell lies." Why? Not just because lying is evil, but because as a pure intellectual judgment it is self-contradictory. If everyone told lies there would be no truth-telling and no one would ever believe any statements at all. In that case lying wouldn't work!

For Kant, the word "categorical" meant the opposite of hypothetical. In a hypothetical proposition you are asked to choose: "If you want to be happy, then you must be good." But Kant wanted ethics to be based on a non-hypothetical obligation of reason, to which the will ought to conform irrespective of individual passions. Whether you are inclined to be honest or not, it is clear that dishonesty is contrary to reason.

Some say that Kant's very philosophically-worded formula can be summarized much more simply in the well-known Biblical injunction: "Do to no one what you would not want done to you" (Tobit 4:15).

Since we have already shown how Kant would deal with lying, let us now turn to the abortion issue which

Lisa and Mark are facing. Here are some of the considerations which might occur to them:

1. Could I will a universal law that all mothers who do not want their babies should abort them?

How could I? Am I sure that I was wanted at the moment of my mother's first knowledge of pregnancy? In case she did not positively want me would I prefer never to have existed?

(How would you, the reader, answer that question?)

2. Could I will the universal law that anyone has a right to kill *anyone* whom he or she doesn't want—even if that person is psychologically harmful? Even in the case of rape, since I condemn the rapist for venting his own torments on an innocent person, should I not condemn myself if I vent on the innocent baby my torment at being pregnant?

3. Can I universalize the proposition that the burden of proof should rest on a being to show that he or she is a full person or else be killed; or ought I universalize the proposition that any potential person has value...?

4. If I say that all handicapped fetuses should be killed, would I universalize that to say that all less-than-perfect adults should be killed? Would I think *I* should be killed if I lost an arm in an auto accident? Should any woman who had a syphilitic husband and had given birth to a stillborn child, a deaf and dumb child, and one with tuberculosis, risk another pregnancy? Beethoven's mother did. Should any woman who is pregnant out of wedlock, has no housing, has no money, and lives in an over-populated area, abort the child? Mary didn't!

5. Would I have wanted my own birth to depend on what year of college my mother was in, or how far along she was in her career?

6. Are these emotional arguments, or do they point to a mystery about life, the sense of which should be universalized?

7. Which proposition would I rather universalize— all unwanted babies should be killed, or all unwanted

babies should be put up for adoption by couples who want a baby?

8. In avoiding accountability for sexual intercourse, am I universalizing the proposition that human beings should use any means to avoid the consequences of their actions?

9. Could I universalize the proposition that all laws that are steadily violated should be taken off the books? If anti-abortion laws, why not anti-speeding laws? No one forces a person to have an abortion if it is against her conscience. No one forces a person to speed.

Now turn to your own ethical dilemma and work out questions which could be asked in terms of the categorical imperative.

Just as Lisa and Mark are about to commit themselves to keeping their baby, a new doubt comes in the form of a question raised in class by a philosophy major.

After learning about ethical intuition, natural law, and the categorical imperative, this young woman argues: "I still can't see how anyone could be absolutely sure something was intrinsically loving or unloving. I'm sure that slave owners thought they were being loving in taking care of their slaves and bringing them the Christian faith. Now we all think they were terribly unloving in their blindness to freedom. Perhaps what we see as good we will later see as evil. I think we can't be sure and shouldn't pretend there is even such a thing as absolute love or lack of love."

Here are some of the ways this student's professor tries to refute her ideas:

"Arguments such as this flow from scepticism and relativism. There are various forms:

"1. No human being is God, so you should not claim to know *anything* with absolute certainty. (Ethical Scepticism)

"2. There are different ideas of right and wrong in other cultures. One should not set up the norms of one's own society as an absolute. Since 500 miles away the people might accept as natural the same act morally frowned upon in our country, we should realize that moral rules are arbitrary.

"George Bernard Shaw argued that morals are mostly only social habits and circumstantial necessities. A. J. Ayer claims that the causes of moral phenomena are psychological rather than ethical. Saying 'thou shalt' is but another way of registering your own desire that the other perform in a certain manner, it has nothing to do with moral absolutes. (Cultural Relativism)

"3. We are all conditioned by economic and historical forces to set up certain values as absolutes, but there is no eternal sanction for any of them. This concept is especially important in Marxist philosophy, as indicated in the complicated but highly interesting quotation from Engels:

> The conceptions of good and bad have varied so much from nation to nation and from age to age that they have often been in direct contradiction to each other.

> But all the same, someone may object, good is not bad and bad is not good: if good is confused with bad there is an end to all morality, and everyone can do and leave undone whatever he cares....

> If it was such an easy business there would certainly be no dispute at all over good and bad; everyone would know what was good and what was bad. But how do things stand today? What morality is preached to us today?

> There is first Christian-feudal morality, inherited from past centuries of faith; and this again has two main subdivisions, Catholic and Protestant moralities, each of which in turn has no lack of further subdivisions from the Jesuit-Catholic and Orthodox-Protestant to loose, 'advanced' moralities. Alongside of these we find the modern bourgeois morality and with it, too,

the proletarian morality of the future, so that in the most advanced European countries alone the past, present and future provide three groups or moral theories which are in force simultaneously and alongside of each other. Which is then the true one? Not one of them, in the sense of having absolute validity....

But when we see that the three classes of modern society, the feudal aristocracy, the bourgeoisie and the proletariat, each have their special morality, we can only draw the one conclusion, that men, consciously or unconsciously, derive their moral ideas in the last resort from the practical relations on which they carry on production and exchange.

But nevertheless there is much that is common to the three moral theories mentioned above—is this not at least a portion of a morality which is externally fixed? These moral theories represent three different stages of the same historical development, and have therefore a common historical background, and for that reason alone they necessarily have much in common. Even more. In similar or approximately similar stages of economic development moral theories must of necessity be more or less in agreement. From the moment when private property in movable objects developed, in all societies in which this private property existed there must be this moral law in common: Thou shalt not steal. Does this law thereby become an eternal moral law? By no means. In a society in which the motive for stealing has been done away with, in which therefore at the very most only lunatics would ever steal, how the teacher of morals would be laughed at who tried solemnly to proclaim the eternal truth: Thou shalt not steal!

We therefore reject every attempt to impose on us any moral dogma whatsoever as an eternal, ultimate and forever immutable moral law on the pretext that the moral world has its permanent principles which transcend history and the differences between nations. We maintain on the contrary that all former moral theories are the product, in the last analysis, of the economic stage which society had hitherto moved in class antagonisms, morality was always a class morality: it has either justified the domination and the interests of the ruling class, or, as soon as the oppressed class has become powerful enough, it has represented the revolt against this domination and the future interests of the oppressed.[5] (Marxist Relativism)

"Having presented in outline the three main standpoints favoring the idea that there are no absolutes—ethical scepticism, cultural relativism, and Marxist relativism—let us now turn to some refutations:

"1. Ethical Scepticism: the theory that we cannot know anything for certain. I hold that even though we cannot know all truth because we are only finite human beings, it is still possible to have some valid insights.

"Look at this list of acts. Put an 'X' next to those you think are certainly wrong and put a '?' next to those you think could be right:

   a) torture an innocent human being
   b) murder an innocent human being
   c) maim a child
   d) cause an innocent friend to go to jail for life
   e) be a spy for an evil group of people who are enslaving one hundred innocent people

---

5. Friedrich Engels, "The Communist Manifesto," from *The Marx-Engels Reader*, ed. Robert C. Tucker (New York: Wm. C. Norton & Co., Inc., 1978), p. 489.

f) rape someone

g) earn your living by setting up a slave system.

"Do you think that you would have to be God in order to be sure about the rightness or wrongness of those acts (a-g)?

"Here is another relevant question: why is it that when we are the victim of a blatant injustice we are perfectly sure that the act was wrong, whereas when we are strongly tempted to do something usually considered wrong, we are quick to invoke as an excuse the idea that there are no moral absolutes? For example, if a teacher gives an unfair grade you don't react by saying—'Maybe her (or she) is right. There are no moral absolutes.' But if you want to cheat you'll most likely deny that cheating is totally wrong.

"2. Cultural Relativism: based on the fact that people in different cultures have varying moral rules. I argue that plurality of rules does not prove that no one rule is better than another. Few really think Nazi Germany's ethics as good as those of post-Nazi Germany.

"Also, it can be argued that even if people of different cultures differ in the application of basic moral ideas to specific cases, most agree on the essence.

"Here are some passages by moral philosophers trying to *refute* relativism in these terms. Underline what strikes you as true and put a question mark next to anything you disagree with:

> Everyone has heard people quarrelling. Sometimes it sounds funny and sometimes it sounds merely unpleasant; but however it sounds, I believe we can learn something very important from listening to the kinds of things they say. They say things like this: 'How'd you like it if anyone did the same thing to you?'— 'That's my seat; I was there first.'—'Come on, you promised....'
>
> Now what interests me about all these remarks is that the man who makes them is not

merely saying that the other man's behavior does not happen to please him. He is appealing to some kind of standard of behavior...some kind of Law or Rule of fair play and decent behavior or morality or whatever you like to call it, about which they really agreed.

Now, this Law or Rule about Right and Wrong used to be called the Law of Nature of Human Nature. The idea was that, just as all bodies are governed by the law of gravitation and organisms by biological laws, so the creature called man also had his law—with the great difference that a body could not choose whether it obeyed the law of gravitation, but man could choose to obey the Law of Human Nature or to disobey it....

Taking the race as a whole, they thought that the human idea of decent behavior was obvious to everyone. And I believe they were right. If they were not, then all the things we said about the war were nonsense. What was the sense in saying the enemy were in the wrong unless Right is a real thing which the Nazis at bottom knew as well as we did and ought to have practiced....

I know that some people say the idea of a Law of Nature...is unsound, because different civilizations and different ages have had quite different moralities.

But this is not true. There have been differences between their moralities, but these have never amounted to anything like a total difference. I need only ask the reader to think what a totally different morality would mean. Think of a country where people were admired for running away in battle, or where a man felt proud of double-crossing all the people who had been kindest to him. You might just as well try to imagine a country where two and two made five...selfishness has never been admired.

But the most remarkable thing is this. Wherever you find a man who says he does not believe in a real Right and Wrong, you will find the same man going back on this a moment later...if you try breaking [a promise] he will be complaining, 'It's not fair....'

It seems, then, we are forced to believe in a real Right and Wrong. People may be sometimes mistaken about them, just as people sometimes get their sums wrong; but they are not a matter of mere tastes and opinions any more than the multiplication table.[6]

—C. S. Lewis

From the diversity of many moral judgments; ...the fact that certain people hold a thing to be morally evil while other people believe the same thing to be morally correct...in no way proves that the object to which the opinion refers does not exist.

The fact that the Ptolemaic system was for centuries considered correct but is now superseded by our present scientific opinion is no justification for denying that the stars exist or even that our present opinion has only a relative value....

The truth of a proposition does not depend upon how many people agree to it, but solely upon whether or not it is in conformity with reality.... Even if all men shared a certain opinion, it could still be wrong, and the fact that very few grasp a truth does not therefore alter or lessen its objective validity....

---

6. C. S. Lewis, *Mere Christianity* (New York: The Macmillan Co., 1943), pp. 17-18.

Sometimes we find that those who are in a rage against the notion of any objective norm and any objective value nevertheless strive against them in the name of 'freedom' or 'democracy'; and thereby they fully admit the character of the value of freedom or democracy. They do not speak of freedom as if it were something merely agreeable or as if they wanted it for personal reasons, but they speak of it as an 'ideal'....[7]

—Dietrich Von Hildebrand

"3. Marxist Relativism: based on the theory that morality reflects the economic conditions of a people rather than an absolute ethical stance.

"Although theoreticians such as Engels claim that morality is no more than an effect of economic conditions, it is impossible for them to actually hold this concept consistently.

"Why?

"Because Communist ideology involves inspiring people in non-Communist countries to revolt in indignation against the moral evils of capitalism. We are supposed to detest the injustice of exploitation of the poor. But how could we truly believe exploitation to be unjust if there is no such thing as justice, if justice is merely a bourgeois concept caused by economic necessity?

"What is more, we are supposed to be motivated by our moral indignation to actually sacrifice our lives and those of others for the victory of the Party. But to sacrifice for the future of the human race presupposes that it is good to altruistically set aside our own legitimate personal desires for the good of others. How can altruism be a virtue if there are no virtues, only economic conditions favoring a false belief that virtues are ethically good?"

---

7. Dietrich Von Hildebrand, Ethics (Chicago: Franciscan Herald Press, 1953), pp. 108ff.

Having heard these refutations, Lisa and Mark feel strengthened against doubt. They realize that at all times it must be wrong to kill an innocent baby. They see that it is value-blindness that makes so many in our culture go along with abortion.

Step IV
Integrating Loving Choices into Your Lifestyle

It is not enough to come to an ethical decision about what is loving and what is unloving.

We also need to bring this choice to reality in terms of our whole life pattern. Some elements to be considered here are:

a) responsibility for what is entrusted to one

b) pursuing one's own legitimate goals

c) continual growth in concern.

Clearly Lisa and Mark, if they keep their baby rather than give it up for adoption (also a very loving choice), will have new responsibilities.

Probably they will decide to give security to each other and to their child by getting married, taking an apartment or house, and building up their finances to take care of these expenses by working, taking out loans, or whatever is possible. They will love this baby and their future babies very much and feel greatly enriched by being parents.

At the same time, they will try to work their own individual career goals into their plans. They may decide that both of them will go part-time to school and work part-time, or Lisa may quit school and work, or Mark might do this for a number of years, until eventually both finish medical school. (I've seen this work.)

The happiest people I know have learned how to balance loving responsibility to others with the self-love necessary for developing and using their own special talents in other areas.

The future happiness of Lisa and Mark will also depend on their continual growth in love, so that they won't fall into the trap of spending so much time on baby and career that they will have nothing left for each other or for their relatives, friends, and patients.

In the case of your own ethical choice, try to work out in writing the elements of responsibility, pursuit of your own goals, and continual growth in love.

Is There a God of Love?

The first three chapters of *Living in Love* are addressed primarily to those readers whose motivations are largely natural and human in origin.

How do questions about living in love change if someone is religious, or specifically Christian?

The word "religion" comes from the Latin *religio*, meaning "bond." A person might have a vague belief that there is a first cause of the universe without being religious. For he or she might not experience a bond with that Cause.

The God of most religions is seen not only as a cause or force, but also as a person—usually not a human person with a body, but nonetheless a consciousness, and especially one who cares about his creatures.

This type of God clearly has importance for decisions about love, for he claims to love us and to want us to grow in ways of his choosing.

Here are some ways in which belief in the existence of a God of Love affects a person's ethical behavior:

—If the ultimate foundation for the universe is its creation out of love by a God of love, then our life goals should be related to love.

—If God thinks love is most important, being a loving person takes precedence over amassing possessions, achieving status or fame, or just "doing your own thing."

—If God loves love and hates indifference, one's eternal destiny might be a result of how much one followed the way of love in time.

—A God of love may have given us commandments on how to live in love which we must follow.

—If there is a God of love, our efforts to procure good for those whom we love do not end in failure because of death. We can live with a horizon of victory over death which prevents ultimate pessimism and the tendency to give up.

In the case of large personal sacrifices entailed by love for others, we know that God wants these and will recompense us.

Let's suppose that Lisa and Mark are taking a course in theology just at the time they are making their decision. Both were brought up as Catholics but at college they dropped away from active participation in worship. They spend so much time concentrating on their studies and on each other that they pray infrequently at best.

In their theology class the great difference is pointed out between believing in God as an *Impersonal Cause* and believing in him as a *Personal Cause*. They realize that their type of belief will make a difference in their decision about their baby. Is this a matter of simply their own private decision?

They are not absolutely sure that God is love, and perhaps some readers are NOT so sure either.

Here is the reasoning of Dr. Stephen Schwarz, a Catholic philosopher and professor teaching at the University of Rhode Island, a secular campus:

"1. What can I do if the existence and non-existence of a God of Love are both uncertain?

"2. Consider the possibilities:

There is a God of Love.   There is not a God of Love.

(A)   (B)

I believe in him.   I do not believe in him.

"In this degree, the top part represents two possibilities regarding the *objective situation*, how it really is. The bottom represents two corresponding positions that can be taken by each *person*. The four lines represent four possible combinations among the four elements of the diagram. Thus:

"3. If there is a God of Love, I should believe in him.

"If there is *not*, I should not believe.

"So much for the vertical lines, which are clear.

"4. But, I may be in error: diagonal lines. Both are tragic in that I am mistaken. I have been deluded. I have made the wrong commitment. But from this point of view (truth) they are equal.

"5. Leaving aside the viewpoint of truth, where they are equal, how do A and B compare otherwise?

"6. Line A is tragic because I am fooled—I wasted my time believing in a God who doesn't exist.

"7. Line B? Isn't this an *infinitely greater tragedy*? There *was*, after all, Infinite Love waiting for me, with consolation for all my sufferings, with salvation from the evils and absurdities of life. There *was* Love and I ignored him. Truly my life was wasted. How much worse to be wrong in this way!

"8. And perhaps the God of Infinite Love has prepared an eternity of happiness for those who respond to him. Can I afford to risk such a loss?

"9. The stakes are great if there is a God of Love: the loss or gain of an infinity, an eternity of happiness.

"10. But really the deepest and greatest tragedy of B is not my loss, here and afterwards, but that I have failed to give the *response due to Infinite Love.* How tragic when *human* love is rejected, how much more when Infinite Love is rejected."

Now that I realize how much is at stake, I ought to seek to find out if there is a God of Love. This can be done through reasoning, through questioning others who believe, through making contact with God in prayer.

Schwarz argues that if we seek God then we have to decide whether to trust experiences which seem to show that there is a God of Love. Failure to seek or trust is tragic for us. Not only does it shut the door on such infinite love, but also we will be unable to give the due response.

Let's say that Lisa and Mark study the traditional arguments for the existence of God and also return to prayer. They come to a stronger sense of a living God.

Love in the Gospels

Lisa and Mark start to read the New Testament in an effort to recover something of the faith they had before.

Certain main truths become clearer with implications for ethics:

We Belong to God

In the religious vision of the meaning of life, we are not seen as merely material entities thrown by chance into the world, but rather as sons and daughters of a loving Father who, therefore, deserves our obedience.

St. Paul writes in his letter to the Ephesians: "He chose us in him before the foundation of the world, that we should be holy and blameless before him" (Ephesians 1:4).

And in the letter to the Romans it is written: "None of us lives to himself, and none of us dies to himself. If we live, we live to the Lord, and if we die, we die to the Lord; so then, whether we live or whether we die, we are the Lord's" (Romans 14:7-8).

The Catholic theologian, Hans Urs Von Balthasar, writes: "God and God alone, has the right to demand all from man because His word is salvation and demands only in order better to give." [1]

The Protestant theologian, Dietrich Bonhoeffer, explains in his book *Ethics:* "The question in ethics for the believers is not how can I be good or do good but what is God's will. If it is the first two questions, then I and the world would be the center, not God. But God is the ultimate reality.... What is central in Christian ethics is that God became Christ. The question is not the relationship between is and ought, motive and act, but rather participation in Christ. Since only God is good, it is only by sharing in Him that we become good." [2]

God Blesses Goodness

God loves and cares for us. He has prepared for us an eternal kingdom of bliss. Therefore we ought to be willing to sacrifice earthly fulfillment if it conflicts with the needs of others—that man may not be the victim of man.

Very often when we are asked to make very difficult sacrifices we are tempted to imagine that the Church is heartless in demanding so much. And it *would be* terribly harsh of God to insist that we give up all hope for human happiness for the sake of the good of others. The invitation to lay down our lives for others (see John

---

1. *A Theological Anthropology* (New York: Sheed & Ward: 1967).
2. *Op. cit.,* pp. 188ff.

15:13) contains the promise of our own personal fulfillment through divine love. How else could Jesus admon-
ish us with the words: "What good is it for a man to gain
the whole world, yet forfeit his soul?" (Mark 8:36–NIV)

It is through an ever-deepening appreciation of
God's love that we are able to accept the seeming impos-
sibility of the Christian doctrine that it is better to suffer
than to sin. We are willing to take up the cross because
we are following him through the cross to the resurrection.

The Struggle Between Good and Evil

Because of the nature of our fallen humanity, the
choice between egoism (the worldly spirit) and sacrificial
love involves a terrible struggle.

Being seduced by worldly values means being sensual, acquisitive, complacent, defensive, proud, con-
temptuous, fawning, possessive, irritable and vengeful,
whereas: "The fruit of the Spirit is love, joy, peace,
patience, kindness, goodness, faithfulness, gentleness,
self-control" (Galatians 5:22-23).

"Do not be conformed to this world but be trans-
formed by the renewal of your mind, that you may prove
what is the will of God, what is good and acceptable and
perfect" (Romans 12:2).

We are not allowed, as Christians, to settle into a
compromise position. God does not say, "Be a nice guy,
be a nice gal," but he calls to us with a voice thundering
yet thrilling: "You shall love the Lord your God with all
your heart, and with all your soul, and with all your
mind.... You shall love your neighbor as yourself" (Matthew 22:37, 39).

The reader should now read the New Testament,
especially the Gospels and Letters, and make notes regarding:

1) Which instances and words show how loving
Jesus was? Which show his knowledge of the lovingness
of God the Father?

2) Which virtues are lauded and which vices condemned?

3) Which attitudes and deeds are considered loving and which unloving?

To follow Christ, however, depends on strongly believing that he is a supreme authority.

Several people in the theology class Lisa and Mark are attending doubted whether it could be shown that Christ was divine.

The professor brought in the classical argument of C. S. Lewis in *The Case for Christianity:*

The argument Lewis presents is extremely simple. There are three possibilities if a man claims to be divine:

a) he is a liar
b) he is a psychotic
c) he really is divine.

Christ appears in the Gospels as an extremely good and truthful person. Far from being judged insane, he is held by many as the best man who ever lived, so there is good reason to take his claim very seriously. Otherwise we would be in the absurd position of saying that the most admirable man who ever lived made the most absurd claims ever!

Doubters have found two main arguments for avoiding these alternatives:

1) Christ did not claim to be divine; disciples and commentators made this assertion later.

2) Christ's claim to be divine was only a way of saying that every man is divine.

To the first statement it can be replied that, in the context of Hebrew thought, to call oneself the Son of God is to claim divinity, and that the Jewish leaders condemned Christ precisely for this assertion, which they thought to be blasphemy.

Regarding the second contention—that Christ was only telling us that we are all divine—it must be noted that Jesus continually emphasized forgiveness of sin. It is incoherent to claim that Christ came to forgive the sins of men if he was actually trying to tell these same men that they were divine. Furthermore, instead of teaching them to follow him—to believe that he is the way, life, and truth—he would have taught them to seek the divine within themselves if he had believed that all men were equally divine.

Now we will do a swift playback over the ideas about virtue in our chapter on becoming a loving person to see how love of God in Christ transfigures virtues and vices.

In a famous passage St. Augustine has given us a way to understand this:

"Virtue [is] nothing else than perfect love of God. For the fourfold division of virtue, I regard as taken from four forms of love...temperance is love giving itself entirely to that which is loved; fortitude is love readily bearing all things for the sake of the loved object; justice is love serving only the loved object, and therefore ruling rightly; prudence is love distinguishing with sagacity between what hinders it and what helps it. The object of this love is not anything, but only God, the chief good, the highest wisdom, the perfect harmony. So we may express the definition thus; that temperance is love keeping itself entire and incorrupt for God; fortitude is love bearing everything readily for the sake of God; justice is love serving God only, and therefore ruling well all else, as subject to man; prudence is love making a right distinction between what helps it towards God and what might hinder it." [3]

Relating to virtues and vices, think how respectful and direct toward others Jesus was and taught his followers to be (see Matthew 5:1-15; Luke 7:36-50).

---

3. St. Augustine, "The Morals of the Catholic Church," *Basic Writings of St. Augustine*, translated by R. Sotohert (New York: Random House, 1948), pp. 331-332.

Consider the constant command in the Old and New Testaments to be generous rather than greedy (see Proverbs 15:6, 16-17, 27; Matthew 6:28-32; 10:8-9; 19:20-24; Mark 12:41-44; Luke 12; 16:19-31; James 2:14-17).

How often Jesus mentions peace and condemns the contempt that reigns in anger (see Mark 9:50; Luke 2:14; 19:42; John 14:27; Matthew 5:21-24).

Purity is revered and lust is condemned (see Exodus 20:14; Proverbs 6:32; Matthew 5:27-28; 15:19; Romans 13:9).

Concerning the *Steps in Making Loving Decisions,* a Christian perspective can be decisive in strengthening the resolve to avoid evil for the sake of love.

Far from laying down survival as a legitimate reason for transgression, Jesus says we should lay up treasures in heaven (Matthew 6:19-21). We should seek first the kingdom of heaven. It is the devil, "the father of lies" (John 8:44), who would urge Lisa and Mark to kill their baby because they could not live with the burden of parenthood. In a Christian philosophy sin is seen as worse than any suffering.

Christian doctrine can also play a clarifying role in cases when conscience is used as an excuse.

In Christianity the problem of conscience cannot be separated from the doctrine of man's original fall. We do not have a pure nature which seeks only the good. Our minds are often too clouded by egocentricity for us to be sure that what we believe to be good at a given moment is really what is objectively good or what corresponds to God's will. Our fallen nature tips the scales.

Since the Fall many plans which seem very right to us, as the proverb states, turn out to be ways of death. In other words, our conscience can be erroneous even when we intend no direct malice.

Human beings are such that we can easily become so caught up in a particular worldly pattern, such as wealth and greed, or the success goal in school, that no intervention of God, no matter how powerful, not even the resurrection of the dead, not even the words of Christ himself, can penetrate through a web of excuses we can place in the way of an ethical breakthrough.

In terms of the teaching of the Catholic Church, it is our doctrine that a person has to follow his or her conscience even if it might later prove to be erroneous. However, we are to search our consciences to make sure that they correspond to what is objectively right and wrong in the light of Christ. We are not allowed to let our consciences be formed merely by fear of earthly punishment, approval of people around us, or self-chosen principles which may be compromises with our own vices.

The Bible never goes along with the popular excuse: "Everybody's doing it." God's will may be and usually is opposite to what most people say.

"An evildoer listens to wicked lips; and a liar gives heed to a mischievous tongue" (Proverbs 17:4).

"Why does the way of the wicked prosper? Why do all who are treacherous thrive?" (Jeremiah 12:1)

"If a blind man leads a blind man, both will fall into a pit" (Matthew 15:14).

"And Pharisees came up to him and tested him by asking, 'Is it lawful to divorce one's wife for any cause?' He answered, 'Have you not read that a man shall leave his father and mother and be joined to his wife, and the two shall become one? So they are no longer two but one. What therefore God has joined together, let no man put asunder.' They said to him, 'Why then did Moses command one to give a certificate of divorce, and to put her away?' He said to them, 'For your hardness of heart Moses allowed you to divorce your wives, but from the beginning it was not so'" (Matthew 19:3-8).

The Scripture is characterized by a very strong dichotomy between "the world" and "the kingdom of God." Worldly ways always seem to prosper. They always attract the majority. There is always a struggle against their magnetism, since they appeal to our natural desire for survival.

For this reason, the counsel of the wicked is to be avoided, since it will always justify wrongdoing and condemn goodness as naive. The wicked worldly ones are alert to their own advantage in terms of immediate gain but are blind to true morality.

In the famous passage from Matthew just quoted, we see how worldliness can become part of the law, accepted even by the most righteous, the Pharisees. Such "upright" ones will cling to the law instead of getting to the essence of right and wrong. Jesus accuses them of ignoring God's law of creation, and God's will for unbreakable unity between man and wife, in favor of giving in to the worldliness which judges fidelity impossible to bear.

If Lisa and Mark were to decide for abortion their act would be within the letter of the state law, according to the ideas held by progressive leaders in the community, but contrary to God's law, which has written creativity, not destruction, into the nature of sexual union between man and woman.

Scripture also highlights the tendency to think there are no victims when there really are:

"Am I my brother's keeper?" (Genesis 4:9)

"You have heard that it was said to the men of old, 'You shall not kill; and whoever kills shall be liable to judgment.' But I say to you that every one who is angry with his brother shall be liable to judgment; whoever insults his brother shall be liable to the council, and whoever says 'You fool!' shall be liable to the hell of fire" (Matthew 5:21-22).

I have picked out these passages because they indicate so vividly that things from which we would like to excuse ourselves can be very grave. What could be worse than murdering a brother, and yet Cain had the gall to reply to God's questioning with the famous words: "Am I my brother's keeper?" What could seem to us a more trivial sin than insulting someone, and yet Jesus considered this a terrible outrage, a stinging blow to the kingdom of love he had come to establish.

From the Christian perspective we should be so close to others—loving them as ourselves, with that kind of solidarity we feel with our very selves—that we would consider their interests to be as important as our own.

If this were the case we would see victims everywhere whenever we make the slightest wrong step, instead of rationalizing that no one is a victim unless there is a scream.

If you recall, Lisa's last excuse in the version of our tale where she opted for the abortion was: "Nobody's perfect."

Here we find Christianity both more stringent and more merciful than natural judgments.

"You cannot serve God and mammon" (Matthew 6:24).

"Because you are lukewarm and neither cold nor hot, I will spew you out of my mouth" (Revelation 3:16).

"The scribes and the Pharisees brought a woman who had been caught in adultery.... Jesus...said to them, 'Let him who is without sin among you be the first to throw a stone at her'...and Jesus was left alone with the woman standing before him.... 'Has no one condemned you?'.... 'Neither do I condemn you; go, and do not sin again'" (John 8:3-11).

On the one hand we have Christ demanding a choice for perfection, insisting that we overcome our lukewarm mediocre tendencies to compromise in order to adhere to the most extraordinary ideals proposed to weak human nature. All this is to be done with the help of God, for whom all things are possible.

On the other hand, the same Christ doesn't want us to set ourselves up as harsh judges over each other. Each of us should aim for the highest, but we should be merciful to the sinner, for we ourselves know how weak we are and how tempting wrongdoing can be. This contradicts the phrase often heard among non-religious people: "I could never forgive this."

Notice also that in the story of Jesus and the woman caught in adultery the woman is totally humble. She doesn't defend herself with false bravado, claiming that her sin can be justified. And by forgiving her Jesus doesn't lower the ideal. He tells her to go and sin no more, thereby reasserting the ideal of marital fidelity and the sinfulness of adultery.

It seems to me that all this may be summed up by a famous phrase of St. Augustine's: "Hate the sin, love the sinner." We must aim for perfection and hate our own sinfulness but at the same time we are to be merciful to ourselves and others as poor, weak, sinful creatures.

If Lisa and Mark had chosen abortion, the mercy of Christ would always have been there when they repented.

Have these Gospel perspectives helped you with your own ethical dilemma? Note your response.

The Holy Spirit as Guide in the Ethics of Love of the Catholic Church

Many Christians who accept the teachings of Jesus in a general way are reluctant to see the teachings of the Church as definitive.

These teachings purport to be based on Scripture, doctrine and tradition, but there are difficulties everywhere.

Some think it is childish to agree with blind faith to Christian moral injunctions. Instead, they hold, we should think everything out personally.

Some find seeming contradictions within Scripture or between particular passages and traditional Church doctrines.

There is a great tension between fundamentalist interpretations of Scripture on the one hand and extremely "liberal" symbolic interpretations on the other, sometimes within the same Church, community or family. Many moderate people conclude that the safe middle course is to use their own judgment, following the spirit rather than the letter.

Many moral pronouncements in Scripture or from the pulpit, the Pope or Councils, seem so hard to apply to modern life that some "believers" assume that these ethical demands are exaggerations or ideals for the already holy. Shouldn't future changes be anticipated by adopting modern views that are more sensible and livable than the harsh pronouncements of Scripture and tradition?

In spite of such apparently plausible and very widespread reasons why many tend to rely solely on personal judgment in moral decision-making without submitting to any higher scriptural or doctrinal authority, it is very hard to square such an individualistic stance with the basic truths about human nature and Christian truth. Can a person be said to belong to God who ignores God's views except when these happen to coincide with his or her own? Given our weak nature, don't we need an objective admonishment from the Lord?

In the book of Proverbs (28:26) we find the terrifying line: "He who trusts in his own mind is a fool; but he who walks in wisdom will be delivered." The Protestant theologian, Bonhoeffer, quoted earlier, points out that, whereas for the natural man conscience is the call to unity with self, for the Christian, unity is to be found only in surrender of the ego to God.[1]

It is interesting to find in a novel written by an agnostic (Iris Murdoch's The Bell) a pithy contemporary admonishment containing the basic truth about man's need to submit humbly to doctrine:

"We should think of our actions and look to God and his Law. We should consider not what delights us or what disgusts us, morally speaking, but what is enjoined and what is forbidden. And this we know, more than we are often ready to admit. We know it from God's Word

---

1. *Ethics*, pp. 243-245.

and from his Church with a certainty as great as our belief. Truthfulness is enjoined, the relief of suffering is enjoined, adultery is forbidden, sodomy is forbidden. And I feel that we ought to think quite simply of these matters, thus: truth is not glorious, it is just enjoined; sodomy is not disgusting, it is just forbidden. These are rules by which we should freely judge ourselves and others too. All else is vanity and self-deception and flattering of passion.... The good man does what seems right, what the rule enjoins, without considering the consequences, without calculation or prevarication, knowing that God will make all for the best. He does not amend the rules by the standards of this world."[2]

In view of the gravity of the crisis among many believers regarding whether to accept doctrine and tradition as a check on one's own ethical reasoning, I will try to present the issue in still another light for your consideration.

In order to understand the controversial topic of moral authority in the Church, *especially as it pertains to Catholic moral authority,* I would like to begin with a reflection on the famous *Myth of the Cave* devised by Plato in his dialogue, *The Republic,* centuries before the birth of the Catholic Church.

Here is Plato's mythical image: There is a dark cave in which prisoners have been chained to the floor, able to face only one wall. Behind them there is a fire blazing at a distance, which casts onto the wall their own shadows and those of people passing by on a walkway behind them. Never having seen their own bodies or the forms of the citizens of the outside world, these prisoners imagine that only shadows are real.

Next Plato asks us to imagine that one of these prisoners breaks free and sees the other people in the cave and finally emerges from the cave and sees free people, the stars and the sun.

---

2. Iris Murdoch, *The Bell* (New York: Penguin Books, 1987).

This is Plato's image of the wise man—the philosopher. Whereas most men on earth see only physical things, the enlightened philosopher sees the intangible element of the world, the souls of men and the truths about being. Ordinary men count shadows and pride themselves at their skill in this (Gallup Poll?) but the wise man looks for more essential truths.

To continue the image of the cave, Plato remarks that if the free man comes back into the cave, his fellow prisoners will by no means automatically believe his visions of the outside world and of their own true natures, especially because the man of light will find it hard to see in the dark anymore and will lack skill in counting the shadows. The analogy is to the attitude the ordinary man takes toward the philosopher. He regards this "wise man" as having his head in the clouds and not understanding the real facts of survival—to lapse into contemporary language. Thus the philosopher will probably be able to enlighten only a few, since the rest will not listen and will not even want to dwell in the light, preferring to rest, secure in their chains.

What would you have done if you were a character in Plato's myth? Would you have been the one who left the cave? On his return, would you have followed him out or would you have remained with the shadow-counters?

I would like to note in regard to similar situations three interesting conclusions that can be drawn from Plato's myth:

1. The freed prisoner who left the cave could be right about the world outside, even if he were one against a hundred in the ideas he held to be true.

2. The freed prisoner could be an idiot in shadow-counting or even a "bad guy" and still be right about the essential truths of the outside world as against the opinions of brighter shadow-counters and better people.

3. The people in the cave could be convinced that they were right, but they might not be right.

Now, let us leave Plato's fascinating myth for a while and turn to an image as strange as his. Do you recognize this:

"Before the world was created, the Word already existed; he was with God, and he was the same as God.... Through him God made all things; not one thing in all creation was made without him. The Word was the source of life, and this life brought light to men. The light shines in the darkness, and the darkness has never put it out....

"The Word was in the world...yet the world did not recognize him. He came to his own country, but his own people did not receive him. Some, however, did receive him and believed in him; so he gave them the right to become God's children....

"Grace and truth came through Jesus Christ. No one has seen God. The only Son, who is the same as God and is at the Father's side, he has made him known" (John 1:1-5, 10-12, 17-18–TEV).

It is striking to note the similarity and differences between the imagery of the Prologue to the Gospel of St. John given here and the Myth of the Cave. Christianity is the fulfillment of Plato's vision. Whereas in Plato's philosophy man must make a tortuous ascent up the mountain of wisdom in order to find truth, in Christianity God descends downward with his message of love and promise of eternal happiness.

When Christ was departing from the apostles just after the Resurrection he said: "I am telling you the truth: it is better for you that I go away, because if I do not go, the Helper [the Holy Spirit] will not come to you. But if I do go away, then I will send him to you. And when he comes, he will prove to the people of the world that they are wrong about sin, and about what is right.... I have much more to tell you, but now it would be too much for you to bear. When, however, the Spirit comes... he will lead you into all the truth..." (John 16:7-8, 12-13–TEV).

In fact, many people who discover a deeper relationship to the Holy Spirit in their lives, find that in a closer
bond to the Spirit many things that they took for granted
as being all right are really un-Christian. Furthermore,
Christ tells the apostles that they are to remain in the
world but not be of the world, and that he will guide
them. He singles out Peter to be the head, and enjoins
them to seek *unity through truth*. (How different Christ's
emphasis is than those of individualism and scepticism!)
We realize the importance of leadership in the Spirit very
soon in the description of matters in the early Church.
Disputes arise about rituals concerning food and circum-
cision. These are solved by direct visions given to Peter
and by a Council during which Peter is convinced by
Paul, but Peter gives the final assent.

To return for a moment to the Myth of the Cave, we
could say that God himself enters the cave with a new
message about the transcendent world and also about
how to transform conditions in the cave. Some follow
him—the disciples. These are like torchbearers. Many
refuse to follow. As with the cave, it is easy to see that
truth cannot be a "numbers game." Peter is right in
following Christ even though public opinion is totally
against him. It is right to follow Peter, even though Peter
is not a genius. Peter doesn't even appear at first to be
any sort of great hero, and yet he is still the true torchbearer, as against some very worthy man who might not
follow Christ at all. As in the case of the cave, many who
did not follow Christ or Peter were convinced that they
were right, but the sincerity of their conviction did not
make them right.

The significance of the comparison that has been
drawn between Plato's cave and Christ's Church will
become still clearer as we now proceed to leap into the
20th century and describe four typical stances taken by
Catholics in the sphere of authority and morality. I am
sure you will recognize these positions. As you read
them you might check the one that comes closest to your

own initial viewpoint and then see if you have reason to question this position as you read on.

1. Unquestioned fidelity: "If the Pope says so it must be so, even if I can't understand it."

2. Faith seeking understanding: "Through reading, thinking and prayer, I have come to see that what the Church teaches really is the truth."

3. Sincere dissent on the basis of conscience: "With regard to one particular doctrine or several doctrines I am convinced that the Church's teaching is wrong, at least for men in our times and in our circumstances, or at least for me in my situation."

4. Rebellious dissent on the basis of selfishness: "I don't care what the Church teaches—nobody can tell me what to do! I'll make my own mistakes, if they are mistakes. I have to go my own way."

Let us examine each of these positions a little more closely, taking the issue of abortion as an example.

1. Unquestioning fidelity to the Church's teachings:

At first sight it may seem that a person who holds such a position is just an uneducated, mindless idiot. But when we look a little closer, this attitude is not so absurd. Such a person might feel this way: "People can argue forever and not get anywhere.... You can find arguments on any side in any dispute. It's a good thing that Christ established a Church to bring light into the confusion of our minds. Throughout my life of prayer and experience I have come to see over and over again how right the Church is, and so I conclude that it makes sense to trust her voice even if it involves sacrifices." A very good case can be made for the fact that Christ wanted his followers to go out and love their neighbors, not to sit and debate issues. He gives different individuals different ministries to his people, and unity can only be achieved by having one supreme leader to enunciate his will in the midst of dispute.

To use an analogy: Suppose you are going on a mountain-climbing trip. You know very little about the mountain, but you have a leader who has been to the top very often. You trust him. You may even have blind confidence in him if you know he is the best guide in the world. Now you come to a certain point in the climb where it seems obvious to you that one path would be best but the guide chooses another path—will you follow him, or your own ideas?

One should note that probably a person would follow this expert guide up the mountain even if the guide had ridiculous political views and six mistresses and got drunk after each excursion.

Now, to apply the analogy. According to Catholic faith, the Holy Spirit is the absolute expert guide in the moral and doctrinal aspect of faith. The Holy Spirit guides all believers, but in the case of dispute, the Spirit speaks through the consecrated leader of the Church, the Pope. Even if some Pope is an immoral man in certain respects, as has happened in the past (the recent Popes have been very holy), or has very questionable political views, when he speaks solemnly to the whole Church he is the torchbearer of the Spirit and should be followed.

A believer with unquestioning fidelity to the Church's teachings on abortion would take as absolutes the scriptural and doctrinal statements on the general subject of destroying the innocent and their application to the unborn child.[3]

Here are some of the relevant statements:

"Cain said to Abel his brother, 'Let us go out to the field.' And when they were in the field, Cain rose up against his brother Abel, and killed him. Then the Lord said to Cain, 'Where is Abel your brother?' He said, 'I do not know; am I my brother's keeper?' And the Lord said,

---

3. For references to statements throughout Church history condemning abortion at every stage of growth, see John A. Hardon, *The Catholic Catechism* (Garden City: Doubleday, 1975), pp. 338-341.

'What have you done? The voice of your brother's blood is crying to me from the ground'" (Genesis 4:8-10).

"Whoever sheds the blood of man, by man shall his blood be shed; for God made man in his own image" (Genesis 9:6).

"Do not slay the innocent and righteous" (Exodus 23:7).

"Cursed be he who slays his neighbor in secret" (Deuteronomy 27:24).

"Children are a gift from the Lord; they are a real blessing" (Psalm 127:3–TEV).

"You created my inmost being;
    you knit me together in my mother's womb....
My frame was not hidden from you
    when I was made in the secret place.
When I was woven together in the depths of the
        earth,
    your eyes saw my unformed body.
All the days ordained for me
    were written in your book
    before one of them came to be."

(Psalm 139:13-16–NIV)

"The Lord called me from the womb;
    from the body of my mother he named my
        name....
And now the Lord says,
    who formed me from the womb to be his
        servant..." (Isaiah 49:1, 5).

"Before I formed you in the womb I knew you,
    and before you were born I consecrated you..."
(Jeremiah 1:5).

"And when Elizabeth heard the greeting of Mary, the babe leaped in her womb; and Elizabeth was filled with the Holy Spirit and she exclaimed.... 'When the voice of your greeting came to my ears, the babe in my womb leaped for joy'" (Luke 1:41-42, 44).

"Do you not know that your body is a temple of the Holy Spirit within you, which you have from God? You are not your own; you were bought with a price. So glorify God in your body" (1 Corinthians 6:19, 20).

"Yet woman will be saved through bearing children, if she continues in faith and love and holiness, with modesty" (1 Timothy 2:15).

"Whatever is opposed to life itself, such as any type of murder, genocide, abortion, euthanasia or willful self-destruction, whatever violates the integrity of the human person...all these things and others of their like are infamies indeed. They poison human society but they do more harm to those who practice them than those who suffer from the injury. Moreover, they are a supreme dishonor to the Creator."[4]

2. "Faith seeking understanding":

I have placed this phrase in quotation marks because it was the main way in which medieval man described the quest of Catholic philosophers. Some Catholics can rest perfectly content with simple fidelity. Most educated Catholics, however, seek to really appreciate why a given doctrine is held to be true. Even an uneducated person will try to ponder why the Church holds certain positions, especially if he or she finds the position obscure.

For example, in the case of a moral principle such as the condemnation of abortion, a relatively uneducated woman might question it before she became a mother, but then when she, herself, experiences the miracle of childbirth, she will understand in a deeply personal way that from the very start the new being in her is a little person, an almost invisible but real little one living within her womb. From the moment of conception the possibility of the child may fill her with awe. She will then shrink from abortion, not only because the Church

---

4. Second Vatican Council, *Pastoral Constitution on the Church in the Modern World* (Boston: St. Paul Editions, 1966), n. 27.

teaches that it is wrong, but also because she understands that it is wrong. The more educated woman will be able to describe the way in which all the elements of life exist as seed in the newly conceived fetus, etc. She will be able to speak about the spiritual dimension of the new creature which cannot be measured in terms of its physical development. She might regard those who allow abortion—depending on the months of development of the fetus—as being like the shadow-counters in Plato's cave who are simply blind to the true meaning of a new human person.

3. Dissent for sincere reasons of conscience:

The Second Vatican Council reaffirmed the traditional teaching of the Catholic Church that even in the case of an erroneous conscience, a person must act in accordance with his or her own judgment.[5]

This doctrine can be viewed as especially relevant to matters concerning religious and political liberty—for example, the civil rights of persons of other religions living in Catholic countries.

The passage has been quoted extensively, however, not so much in connection with tensions between Church and State as with regard to dissent on such controversial issues as birth-control, the subject of the famous encyclical, *Humanae Vitae*.

In the explanation of dissent from the teaching of the Church on artificial contraception, the concept of the sincere conscience of the many Catholics using such methods as the "pill" was brought into prominence. Here the good conscience of the sincere dissenter would consist in his or her summation of moral intuitions and arguments, usually accompanied by prayerful opening to God's will.[6] "Surely the Holy Spirit also speaks to the

---

5. See *Church in the Modern World*, n. 16.

6. For a thorough and penetrating analysis of situation ethics and Catholic teaching, see Dietrich Von Hildebrand, *Morality and Situation Ethics* (Chicago: Franciscan Herald Press, 1982).

faithful Catholic seeking moral guidance as well as to the Pope?'' the dissenter reasons.

What is much more obvious now than when dissent on the birth-control issue began, is that the same reasoning would be used with many other issues, often to the horror of the original proponents of "sincere dissent."

What is certainly true in the emphasis on conscience in contemporary Catholic thought is that guilt is greatly mitigated when there is a sincere, if erroneous, conscience. An unwed teenager who decides that an abortion is the only route to take, because she is frightened to death of potential parental actions administered to a boyfriend who has fled from the scene, is certainly less guilty than a doctor who is running an abortion mill solely for the sake of greater profit than his previous medical activities provided him.

Knowing how much suffering can go into making difficult moral decisions, and horrified at the harshness of judgment sometimes leveled against the sinful by so-called "decent" people who have never faced such a crisis, many religious educators have tended to focus on the authenticity of conscience of the moral agent as if the pain could make a wrongdoing become right. Instead of following Augustine's maxim of "Hate the sin; love the sinner," they "accept the sin, out of love for the sinner."

While showing the utmost understanding and compassion for those caught in moral dilemmas, I believe that it is part of being loving to communicate the wisdom of objective Christian doctrine. Christ and the Holy Spirit, teaching through the Church, would not forbid an act unless it was truly harmful. Knowing how blinded someone may be who is passionately involved in the outcome of a decision, the priestly, pastoral, or educational minister must be the one to shed light on the wisdom of the doctrine in question, rather than yield to the erroneous conscience of the person seeking advice.

Another passage from the *Documents of Vatican II* helps balance the picture of how conscience and doctrine work together. "Conscience is the most secret core and sanctuary of a man. There he is alone with God, whose voice echoes in his depths. In a wonderful manner conscience reveals the law which is fulfilled by love of God and neighbor.... Hence the more that a *correct* conscience holds sway, the more persons and groups turn aside from blind choice and strive to be guided by *objective norms of morality*...recognizing the imperatives of the divine law through the mediation of conscience."[7]

What distinguishes a Catholic conscience from that of a person whose ethics are formed by philosophical considerations alone is the conviction that the Holy Spirit is guiding the teaching authorities of the Church infallibly in matters of faith and morals. Unity of truth is a great gift of the Spirit to the Church, so that making a subjective idea of one's own into an absolute would have to be a denial of Catholic truth.

In our times, when there is a great problem of dissent in the Catholic Church, a Catholic cannot simply trust the views of a teacher or a priest but should consult Scripture, books such as *The Documents of Vatican II*, ed. by Austin Flannery, O.P. (Boston: St. Paul Editions); *The Code of Canon Law* (Washington, D.C., Canon Law Society of America, 1983); *The Church Teaches* (St. Louis: Herder, 1955) which summarize Council Documents from the beginning of Church history; the Catholic Encyclopedia; and *approved* catechisms such as *The Catholic Catechism* by Rev. John A. Hardon, S.J. (New York: Doubleday, 1975).

4. Dissent on the basis of selfishness:

This is the case when someone has basically decided to "do his or her thing," as against "doing the will of God," but still wants to be part of the Church for reasons of sentimentality, habit, desire for the approval of others or, in the best cases, because in the heart of hearts one knows that he or she is in the wrong and hopes to return to the truth someday.

---

7. *Church in the Modern World*, n. 16.

With regard to your own ethical issue, can you find any Church teaching about it? Note down what you discover.

What will follow is a discussion of several controversial issues in terms of Scripture and tradition. These will be brief but will hopefully lead the reader to explore further. As you read, underline any ideas new to you.

Social Justice

Central problem: minimalism—the idea that Christians can pursue their own individual needs with a minimum of concern for others.

Scripture and Church Teaching:

"Is not this the fast that I choose:
  to loose the bonds of wickedness,
  to undo the thongs of the yoke,
to let the oppressed go free,
  and to break every yoke?
Is it not to share your bread with the hungry...?"
(Isaiah 58:6-7)

In the biblical concordance there are more than 200 listings under *just* and *justice* and thousands of others explaining how important it is to care deeply about the needs of the suffering.

In his excellent catechism the American theologian John A. Hardon gives a very balanced view of how these injunctions can be brought into harmony with the right to private property:

"Pressed on the one side by the evils of unbridled ownership and on the other by the theory that private property leads to abuses and therefore all ownership belongs to the State, the Church in our day has had to steer a clear course between two extremes. It has defended ownership and denounced theft as sinful; but it has also insisted on the rights of society and decried selfish greed as morally wrong.... [The Christian] must respect private ownership as divinely ordained, a right inherent in the human person which means that the seventh and tenth commandments are still as valid as they were when first revealed on Sinai. And he must realize that ownership is not an absolute, but that society too has rights for which the author of man's social nature equally demands recognition...."[8]

The bishops of the Second Vatican Council stated:

"God intended the earth and all it contains for the use of all men and peoples, so created goods should flow fairly to all, regulated by justice and accompanied by charity."[9]

In his Encyclical *The Development of Peoples*, Pope Paul VI summarized and applied the constant teaching of the Church in this regard:

" 'If someone who has the riches of this world sees his brother in need and closes his heart to him, how does the love of God abide in him?' (1 John 3:17) It is well known how strong were the words used by the Fathers of the Church to describe the proper attitude of persons who possess anything toward persons in need. To quote St. Ambrose: 'You are not making a gift of your possessions to the poor person. You are handing over to him what is his. For what has been given in common for the use of all, you have arrogated to yourself. The world is given to all, and not only to the rich.' That is, private property does not constitute for anyone an absolute, un- conditioned right. No one is justified in keeping for his exclusive use what he does not need, when others lack necessities. In a word, according to the traditional doc- trine as found in the Fathers of the Church and the great theologians, the right to property must never be exer- cised to the detriment of the common good. If there should arise a conflict between acquired private rights

---

8. John A. Hardon, *The Catholic Catechism* (Garden City: Doubleday, 1975), pp. 386-389.

9. *Church in the Modern World*, n. 69.

and primary community needs, it is the responsibility of public authorities to look for a solution, with the active participation of individuals and social groups." [10]

The common good may require expropriation. The rich should not divert wealth from their own countries for their own personal advantage.

In the Pastoral Letter of the U.S. Bishops *To Live in Christ Jesus* it is stated that "Law and public policy do not substitute for the personal acts by which we express love for neighbor; but love of neighbor impels us to work for laws, policies and social structures which foster human goods in the lives of all persons." [11]

The same letter spells out some of the injustices flowing from discrimination against women, minorities and the elderly. In this way it seeks to overcome the type of minimalism that sees simply the omission of certain grave sins as proof of moral rectitude, leaving out the clear importance for the Christian of positive acts of justice and charity.

The Pastoral of the U.S. Bishops on the economy further clarifies ways these general principles can be related to problems of our day.

War

Main Problem: Because of nationalism and other causes many Christians fail to see that most wars are unjust and therefore anti-Christian. On the other hand, some Christians insist that total pacifism is the only genuine course.

Scripture and Tradition:

The passages relating to being peaceful are countless. Jesus continually greets others with the words:

---

10. Paul VI, *The Development of Peoples* (Boston: St. Paul Editions, 1967), n. 23.

11. U.S. Bishops' Pastoral Letter, *To Live in Christ Jesus* (Washington: United States Catholic Conference, 1976), p. 23.

"Peace be to you." He proclaims that the peacemakers shall be blessed (Matthew 5:9), and he is called the Prince of Peace (Isaiah 9:6). On the other hand, in the New Testament the role of being a soldier was not looked down upon as evil in itself. Luke reports:

"And the multitudes asked him [John the Baptist] 'What then shall we do?' And he answered them, 'He who has two coats, let him share with him who has none; and he who has food, let him do likewise.' Tax collectors also came to be baptized, and said to him, 'Teacher, what shall we do?' and he said to them, 'Collect no more than is appointed you.' Soldiers also asked him, 'And we, what shall we do?' And he said to them, 'Rob no one by violence or by false accusation, and be content with your wages'" (Luke 3:10-14).

Tradition emphasizes both the intrinsic evil of deliberately killing an innocent person, and the importance of seeking all possible methods to eliminate causes of violence and seek peace; but it also makes it clear that self-defense can be justified, even to the extent of going to war.

Here are some of the main points of the tradition as summarized by John A. Hardon:

"In a world wholly governed by Christian principles, war would be ruled out as at variance with the moral teachings of Christ.... But since Christians are also citizens of secular order in which the exercise of force is sometimes necessary to maintain the authority of the law, the Catholic Church has held that the method of war and the active participation of Christians in it are *on occasion* morally defensible and may even be praiseworthy." [12]

The doctrine of the "just war" was developed to try to distinguish on which occasions Christians could be morally justified in supporting a war. Such criteria include the following: a) based on the authority of the

---

12. *The Catholic Catechism*, pp. 346-351.

lawful government (vs. personal or family vendetta), b) for a just cause (i.e., defense against an unjust aggressor), c) using proper means (not causing terrible suffering with no hope of victory, or directly killing the innocent). "All warfare which tends indiscriminately to the destruction of entire cities or wide areas with their inhabitants is a crime against God and man, to be firmly and unhesitatingly condemned."[13]

A document entitled "The Holy See and Disarmament" further emphasizes that it is criminal to stockpile nuclear weapons designed to wipe out whole populations, even as a threat, especially because the funding of such ventures diverts resources from helping the needy.[14]

It is also part of the tradition to object on the basis of conscience to a given war or to all wars, and no nations may demand blind obedience.[15]

What is more, we are constantly being enjoined to play the role of peacemakers as Jesus preached, doing our best to defuse the causes of war rather than easily conforming to nationalistic propaganda.

The United States Bishops' Pastoral on peace and war adds concepts to this summary helpful for the formation of conscience of Americans.

Euthanasia

Main Problem: Many people wonder whether it is required to sustain life by extraordinary means in cases which involve great suffering or expense. In the case of someone in excruciating pain or born with extreme defects, could not a positive act of ending the life of such a person be more charitable than letting him or her live on?

---

13. *Church in the Modern World*, n. 80.

14. See *The Pope Speaks*, Vol. 22, n. 3 (1977), pp. 243-244.

15. See Pastoral of U.S. Bishops, *To Live in Christ Jesus*, p. 34.

Scripture and Tradition:
"Thou shalt not kill!"

The biblical injunction against killing is supported by the very progressive Greek Hippocratic oath taken by all doctors: "I will neither give a deadly drug to anybody who asks for it, nor will I make a suggestion to this effect."

Direct killing of innocent persons for any reason has always been ruled out in Judeo-Christian morality. (In the case of capital punishment or war it is usually maintained that a person who unjustly kills others forfeits his or her own right to life.) Killing an innocent person, including oneself, is a way of usurping God's power over creation and death. This doctrine was reiterated by Pope Pius XII during Nazi times in response to questions regarding eugenics and genocide.

This doctrine also reflects the religious conviction that every human being is infinitely precious regardless of any consideration of development, race, creed, etc. "Not only does man have intrinsic dignity, but God has inalienable rights. The divine lordship over human life is an article of...faith, namely, 'I believe in God the Father Almighty, Creator of heaven and earth.' As a creature of God, to whom man owes every element of his being, man is entrusted only with the stewardship of his earthly existence. He is bound to accept the life that God gave him, with its limitations and powers; to preserve this life as the first condition of his dependence on the Creator, and not deliberately curtail his time...on earth.... Ours is not mastery but only ministry of our own lives as of the lives of others." [16]

On the other hand the Church teaches that we do not have to use extraordinary means to keep a person alive who is in great pain or who is causing tremendous burdens. What extraordinary and ordinary means consist of varies from age to age and culture to culture. This

---

16. John A. Hardon, *The Catholic Catechism*, op. cit., pp. 331-332.

makes it impossible to apply some neat, exact measure. However, moral theologians normally say that ordinary means are those commonly accepted, readily available, without extreme difficulty in terms of pain and expense. "Means do not have to be used which offer no reasonable hope of benefit." [17]

Divorce

Main Problem: As divorce followed by remarriage has become more and more acceptable in the society around us, many Christians question whether in some cases it might not be the most loving thing to humbly accept the fact that some marriages cause more pain than joy and some couples seem incapable of reconciliation. In such cases should not each person be free to try to make a better life with someone else? Especially should the innocent party who has been deserted or maltreated have to live singly for the rest of his or her life?

Scripture and Tradition:
"It was also said, 'Whoever divorces his wife, let him give her a certificate of divorce.' But I say to you that every one who divorces his wife, except on the ground of unchastity, makes her an adulteress; and whosoever marries a divorced woman commits adultery" (Matthew 5:31-32).

"Have you not read that he who made them from the beginning made them male and female, and said, 'For this reason a man shall leave his father and mother and be joined to his wife, and the two shall become one'?... What therefore God has joined together, let no man put asunder.... For your hardness of heart Moses allowed you to divorce your wives, but from the beginning it was not so" (Matthew 19:4-8).

"Whoever divorces his wife and marries another, commits adultery against her, and if she divorces her

---

17. *Ibid.*, p. 328.

husband and marries another, she commits adultery"
(Mark 10:11-12).

Some interpret Christ's words to imply that in cases
of adultery divorce is allowed. I have always thought that
what is meant by the first passage (Matthew 5:31-32) is
that the person who divorces his wife (under the old
customs of Israel) when she is already herself unchaste,
does not cause her to become an adulteress, whereas if
she is pure and faithful, divorcing her will lead her to
seek another mate in adultery.

The emphasis in the tradition is on the importance
of fidelity to the valid bond of love undertaken in marriage. Marriages can only be annulled if such a valid
bond can be proven never to have existed, as in the case
of those forced to marry, those who do not consummate
their marriages in sexual intercourse due to sexual impo-
tence or, in recent times, those who purposely and consciously exclude the notion of marriage as a bond "till
death do us part."

Of late, due to a greater knowledge of the effect of
certain mental disorders on the freedom of the person,
more marriages are being annulled on the basis of extreme immaturity that made a free-will decision of self-
donation impossible.

A very beautiful summary of Church teaching on
divorce is included in the U.S. Bishops' Pastoral Letter of
1976 from which I now quote:

"Every human being has a need and right to be
loved, to have a home where he or she can put down
roots and grow. The family is the first and indispensable
community in which this need is met. Today, when
productivity, prestige or even physical attractiveness are
regarded as the gauge of personal worth, the family has a
special vocation to be a place where people are loved not
for what they do or what they have but simply because
they are.

"A family begins when a man and woman publicly
proclaim before the community their mutual commitment, so that it is possible to speak of them as one body.

Christ teaches that God wills the union of man and woman in marriage to be lifelong, a sharing of life for the length of life itself.

"The Old Testament takes the love between husband and wife as one of the most powerful symbols of God's love for his people: 'I will espouse you to me forever: I will espouse you in right and in justice, in love and in mercy: I will espouse you in fidelity, and you shall know the Lord.' So husband and wife espouse themselves, joined in a holy and loving covenant.

"The New Testament continues this imagery: only now the union between husband and wife rises to the likeness of the union between Christ and his Church. Jesus teaches that in marriage men and women are to pledge steadfast unconditional faithfulness which mirrors the faithfulness of the Son of God. Their marriages make his fidelity and love visible to the world. Christ raised marriage in the Lord to the level of a sacrament, whereby this union symbolizes and effects God's special love for the couple in their total domestic and social situation.

Jesus tells us that the Father can and will grant people the greatness of heart to keep such pledges of loving faithfulness. The Church has always believed that in making and keeping noble promises of this sort, people can, through the grace of God, grow beyond themselves—grow to the point of being able to love beyond their merely human capacity. Yet contemporary culture makes it difficult for many people to accept this view of marriage. Even some who admire it as an ideal doubt whether it is possible and consider it too risky to attempt. They believe it better to promise less at the start and so be able to escape from marital tragedy in order to promise once again.

"But this outlook itself has increased marital tragedy. Only men and women bold enough to make promises for life, believing that with God's help they can be true to their word as he is to his, have the love and strength to surmount the inevitable challenges of marriage. Such unselfish love, rooted in faith, is ready to forgive when need arises and to make the sacrifices demanded if something as precious and holy as marriage is to be preserved. For the family to be a place where human beings can grow with security, the love pledged by husband and wife must have as its model the selfless and enduring love of Christ for the Church. 'Husbands, love your wives, as Christ loved the Church. He gave himself up for her.'

"Some say even sacramental marriages can deteriorate to such an extent that the marital union dies and the spouses are no longer obliged to keep their promise of lifelong fidelity. Some would even urge the Church to acknowledge such dissolution and allow the parties to enter new, more promising unions. We reject this view. In reality it amounts to a proposal to forego Christian marriage at the outset and substitute something entirely different. It would weaken marriage further, by paying too little heed to Jesus' call to identify ourselves with his redeeming love, which endures all things. Its fundamental difficulty is that it cannot be reconciled with the Church's mission to be faithful to the word entrusted to it. The covenant between a man and woman joined in Christian marriage is as indissoluble and irrevocable as God's love for his people and Christ's love for his Church.

"Since the following of Christ calls for so much dedication and sacrifice in the face of strong, contrary social pressures, Christ's Church has a serious obligation to help his followers live up to the challenge. In worship, pastoral care, education, and counseling we must assist husbands and wives who are striving to realize the ideal of Christ's love in their lives together with their children. Young people and engaged couples must be taught the meaning of Christian marriage. Married couples must have the support and encouragement of the Christian community in their efforts to honor their commitments.

"It remains a tragic fact that some marriages fail. We must approach those who suffer this agonizing experience with the compassion of Jesus himself. In some cases romanticism or immaturity may have prevented them from entering into real Christian marriages.

"But often enough 'broken marriages' are sacramental, indissoluble unions. In this sensitive area the pastoral response of the Church is especially needed and especially difficult to formulate. We must seek ways by which the Church can mediate Christ's compassion to those who have suffered marital tragedy, but at the same time we may do nothing to undermine his teaching concerning the beauty and meaning of marriage and in particular his prophetic demands concerning the indissolubility of the unions of those who marry in the Lord. The Church must ever be faithful to the command to serve the truth in love." [18]

Pre-marital and Extra-marital Sex

Main Problem: Given the tremendous emphasis on pleasure in contemporary society, it is very difficult for people to impose restraints on themselves. Also since many think that marriages should not be entered into before the age of twenty-one or even later, it is thought to be too difficult to restrain sexual impulses until that time. Although all Christians reject free-love, some think that in the case of engaged couples who have to wait a long time for marriage, pre-marital intercourse could be all right. Others think that in the case of marriages involving great difficulties, extra-marital sex might be licit.

Scripture and Tradition:

The scriptural word for pre-marital sex is fornication, and for extra-marital sex—adultery. Some people claim that these matters are not emphasized in Scripture,

---

18. Pastoral of U.S. Bishops, *To Live in Christ Jesus*, op. cit., pp. 14-17.

because they do not realize to what these terms refer. Scripture contains many references which forbid any form of fornication or adultery—see especially the commandment "You shall not covet your neighbor's wife" (Exodus 20:17); the book of Hosea; Matthew 5:27-30; Hebrews 13:1-4; 1 Corinthians 6:9, 18.

Tradition has been very strong on these two temptations. Contrary to some opinions, these doctrines have in no way been changed in recent years. They have been reaffirmed in authoritative documents to the present.[19]

In view of the great difficulty for many in accepting these doctrines, I am appending here some reflections of my own I have found helpful in explaining such matters.

Some Viewpoints on Catholic Sexual Morality

Underlying Catholic sexual morality is to be found a philosophy of sexuality as a physical means of expressing a deep, intimate union of two people in love, open to the creation of a new human being—the child. This love must reach the point of a real giving of the self in the emotional, volitional, and spiritual dimension before its physical expression is justified.

The spectrum of possible situations and attitudes of two people engaging in sexual activity has an enormous range. The possibilities described below are necessarily sketchy and incomplete but still may serve to clear up certain difficulties in understanding the morality of sex.

1. Isolated sex. This term is used by Von Hildebrand in his books In Defense of Purity and Man and Woman. It refers to the type of relationship in which sexuality is isolated from love and is experienced merely as a means

---

19. See Sacred Congregation for the Doctrine of the Faith, Declaration on Certain Questions Concerning Sexual Ethics (Boston: St. Paul Editions, 1976), n. 7ff., and U.S. Bishops' Pastoral, To Live in Christ Jesus, pp. 17-19.

for getting pleasure. It is a typical I-it relationship in which the other partner is viewed as dispensable and as an object, rather than as a unique person lovable and worthy of care and consideration. In such a relationship, it is very clear that the physical giving is completely separate from any emotional and spiritual giving and there is obviously no commitment of the will.

Such a sexual act is immoral, because the sexual sphere is an expression of the intimate depth of the personality rather than a surface dimension which is morally neutral, as eating and sleeping are. Because the sexual sphere is so personal, it is wrong to play games with it or to use it to buy love, popularity, status, etc. The despair that results from pursuing a life given to isolated sexuality is well described by Rollo May in his book *Love and Will*. The reason for this despair is that such a person sees his or her selfhood as something used. He or she throws it away instead of seeing it as something cherished which will engender lasting love. Whereas in the relationship of married love the sexual relationship is part of the I-Thou love directed to the irreplaceable unique being of the other, in isolated sex what is given can be replaced by any other woman or man with the same sexual parts.

2. Sex in the love affair. In such a situation sexuality is given a romantic aura which raises it above the level of isolated sex. Two people feel attracted to each other and hope for a relationship lasting longer than one evening. They relate to each other as individuals rather than as sexual organs and measurements, but their interest in each other has little self-giving on an emotional, spiritual or volitional level. All they give to each other is their passing emotional states—they do not unite their hearts and souls or vow to stay together longer than they happen to give each other pleasure. Such relationships are generally filled with self-deceit, for the persons involved will tell one another that they love each other without believing it, flirt with others at the same time, often try to avoid facing the possibility that one or the other might

meanwhile have become serious about the relationship and therefore be hurt by it. To be convinced that such sexuality is immoral, however, it is necessary to believe that a real I-Thou love is possible and that a person ought to preserve so deep an experience as sex for such a relationship. Most often people engaged in love affairs lack this hope. Sometimes one believes that such an affair reflects real love while the other party is sure that it does not, and in these cases such affairs may leave life-long scars of disillusionment and despair.

3. The engaged couple and sex. Many hold that isolated sex and sex in a love affair are wrong, but that sexual intercourse for the engaged couple is fine because in this case there is a real I-Thou love which is being expressed in the physical sphere. Usually marriage is postponed only for exterior reasons involving finances, family difficulties, decisions about finishing school first, military service, etc.

But does the engaged couple really feel joined in a total I-Thou commitment? The couple will argue that they really are married and certainly don't need a piece of paper to prove it; but is it really true that they have made an interior binding vow and that the certificate or religious ceremony is but a conventional trimming of no deeper significance? That an engagement is not an interior marriage lacking only exterior forms can be seen by asking one simple question: is it a sin to break an engagement? The fact that breaking an engagement is always considered possible and not seen as a divorce proves that no one thinks that an engagement represents the same degree of unity as a marriage. Each person is still free to change his or her mind because of the recognition that this love was not as deep as was originally supposed. Hence the engagement expresses the hope that this love is so great that the couple wishes to spend life together, but this hope is not expressed through a full, irrevocable vow of marriage. In case the young people do not marry they may be thankful for all those exterior obstacles which made them postpone marriage.

4. Marital love and sex. The moment of marriage is one of the most dramatic times in life, because it unites all the aspects of the person in the joining of oneself to another. It is the "hyphen" which joins I-Thou. It makes the couple two in one, as Christ proclaims. Here there is no disparity between the body, the heart, the mind, the will, and the spirit. They wish for this union and do not hold themselves back by placing conditions on their love. This overflow of love into the joining of life on every level is gloriously expressed in the possibility that sexuality may bring about a new person, the fruit of the couple's love.

It is an indication of a couple's lack of readiness for sex in pre-marital sexuality if the fruit of the couple's love is viewed as negative and to be prevented or destroyed or at best is viewed as some kind of disaster. In the case of an unmarried couple, that a human person born of the flesh of the person one most loves could be considered something negative reveals the lack of love hidden within the relationship. If, instead, the couple rejoices in this baby and decides to marry, this reveals that their sexual love was an expression of an I-Thou love.

The essence of the sacrament of marriage is the mutual vow of permanent union. However, the making of the vow in the Church before the witness of the priest is a beautiful symbol of the fact that Catholics who marry receive each other in Christ, in the midst of their spiritual I-Thou relationship to Christ. It also symbolizes a rather subtle metaphysical reality: fundamentally a person does not belong so much to himself or to the people surrounding him as to God, and it is God who gives him or her into the hands of the spouse. In this sense it is also true to say that pre-marital sex is immoral because one's body belongs to one's future husband or wife—it has been destined by God to belong to the one person who will love it and cherish it in a whole, total love. Because it belongs to the future husband or wife, it is not mine to throw away or trade for some advantage or use as a plaything. To use another analogy, one could say that a person's sexuality is like a secret closed garden to which only the ultimate lover is to be given the key. It ought not to be received by the spouse as a garden trampled upon and wasted, full of the weeds of random visitors who did not cherish its flowers but picked them and strolled away.

5. Difficulties. But, you may well ask, if this is God's plan why should it be so difficult to live by such ideals? Why should we have to fight against the lure of isolated sexuality? How can we be asked to wait for the perfect love when we don't know if we will ever find it and meanwhile have overpowering sexual needs and desires and pressures?

Much struggle and despair underlies such questions. It is very difficult to live up to Catholic moral ideals unless one's religious life is deep and concrete. It is then, within the context of a living I-Thou relationship to Christ, that we have the faith in God's providential love which will enable us to postpone immediate longings for the sake of the deeper experience of marital sexual love. Unless we love Christ as intensely as we love those who attract us physically and emotionally, we will not have the strength to live in hope that he will give us the gift of a true love. This is the question: do we want to seek the good things as gifts of his love as he has planned, or do we want to listen to the voices of the majority, which always say that we must grasp the tangible, desired things with both hands before it is too late? Do we "seek first the kingdom of heaven and its justice and all things will be added unto you" (see Matthew 6:33), or do we "look out for number one and let the future take care of itself"?

I think that every time of life calls for the making of a particular decision which is always very difficult but which is the most important thing one can do in order to transcend egoistic norms and become more loving in following Christ. For a child the hardest thing might be to avoid joining gangs or cliques and to be friendly with everyone, even the kid the others make fun of. For the teenager and young adult it might be to believe in the ideal of marital sex when all his friends boast of conquests, or to pass up that Saturday night date if she knows where it would lead to. Later it might be to choose a career which is more worthwhile but pays less; and later on to overcome the discouragement that comes from not having achieved what one had dreamed of in order to value the love of the family and friends more than external success. For others it might be to become part of a difficult good cause or to become a priest, or to remain honest in the midst of corruption.

When we see how easily we fall, should we lower the ideal so that we can be comfortable, or should we ask for forgiveness and start again? It is in the midst of temptations to forsake the ideal that we discover the deepest meaning of Christian truths. We discover our weakness— our desire to clutch onto what promises so much and to turn away from Christ's path, and the reality of his forgiveness, and the miracle of the gifts he sends us, which we find to be so different from what we imagined, so much better!

Contraception

Main Problem: Due to the great difficulty of raising families in cities, the problem of poverty, and many other obstacles, many couples think it unwise to have large families. Of these many are unacquainted with the natural rhythms of the woman's fertile cycle, which when properly understood require only a minimum of abstinence from sexual intercourse to avoid an untimely pregnancy. This state of affairs has made the alternative of artificial contraception more and more attractive to many Christian couples.

Scripture and Tradition:
In The Catholic Catechism, John A. Hardon shows that throughout history many different methods of pre-

venting birth have been used. Such practices were described as "using magic" and "using drugs." (See, for example, Galatians 5:20; Revelation 21:8; 22:15.) Throughout history the Church has condemned such practices over and over again (see Hardon, pp. 368-381), culminating in the Encyclical *Humanae Vitae* in 1968. Again, since this issue is so controversial, I would like to explain it more thoroughly:

A Married Woman's Reflections on Humanae Vitae [20]

"You're the first person I've ever heard defend *Humanae Vitae*," a seminarian told me recently.

Discussions of the famous encyclical still focus very much on the question of *who* is raising points pro or con.

When a priest defends *Humanae Vitae*, his arguments are often dismissed as irrelevant for lack of experience—although if a priest dissents, he is listened to with great respect because of his superior theological training.

When a father defends *Humanae Vitae*, his views are often dismissed as based on a sentimental, idealized portrait of motherhood. However, if a father dissents, he is usually listened to with respect as representing the infallible voice of the laity.

As for mothers, it is taken for granted that most accept contraception: less-educated women on the basis of intuition, and college-trained women as part of a philosophy of self-fulfillment, both seeking freedom from the exhausting burden of one baby after the other. A woman who avoids contraceptive means is often thought of as suffering from "slavish fear" of authority.

In view of the above, could any witness be considered credible in defense of the encyclical?

---

20. An article by this author published by *Faith and Reason, The Journal of Christendom College,* 1978.

Yes, I believe so. As wife, mother and philosopher, I feel that I can draw upon my own experience in the home, the classroom and the Church, to formulate a new objective argument which can appeal to all Catholics, irrespective of their roles in the Church.

The first experiences, fundamental to all the rest, are the traditional ones you would expect to find at peak moments for any woman: the day of my wedding; and the birth of each of my children. It was overwhelming to see the baby who had been nurtured for nine months in my own womb appear before my eyes for the first time.

But even before birth, there is another moment, less often discussed, which is very precious to parents. This is the time of sexual union *with a difference!* The couple knows that it is the fertile time, so that added to the joy of the love union there is the mystical sense of participation in an event which goes beyond the subjective toward the incarnational mystery...a unique new person may be conceived at this moment!

This experience is crucial to a deeper insight into *Humanae Vitae's* description of sex as a divine gift and human life as sacred.[21]

The sense of awe before the experience of conception and childbearing has to be at the center of any feminism worthy of the name—how much more a Catholic feminism! To dwell on the words of Sigrid Undset, the Nobel Prize winning woman writer:

"No other belief can give the people of our day courage to live according to nature and accept the children that God gives them, except this—the belief that every child has a soul which is worth more than...the stars in the heavens, though at times she is near fainting under the shower of the stars."[22]

---

21. See Paul VI, *Humanae Vitae* (Boston: St. Paul Editions, 1968), n. 13.

22. Sigrid Undset, *Stages on the Road* (Ayer Co., Publishers).

With the subjective experience of the miracle of fertility in mind, we are encouraged to penetrate the mystery even further through a bold set of comparisons:

As our Lady was prepared by the Immaculate Conception to be ready at the *sacred time* for the Incarnation of Jesus, making a *sacred space* of her womb...

so, too,

at the *sacred time* of the Mass, through the words of the priest, Christ becomes really present on the *sacred place* of the altar...

so, too,

at the *sacred time* of fertility, through the sexual union of the parents, the life of a new creature begins, making the mother's womb into a *sacred space*.

It is in the light of such religious insights that we must understand *Humanae Vitae's* insistence that sexual union is sacred and not to be violated. Not that the sacredness of fertility cannot be understood without religious belief. Any human being can marvel at it, and humanists of all types do express their awe of creative sexuality. Nonetheless, it must be admitted that in our times the sense of sacredness is being lost as other values are given greater weight; so that a return to the Source of the sacred is necessary to renew our appreciation of its natural forms.

Returning to the analogy of the Mass as the peak experience of the priest, and conception as the highest metaphysical fulfillment of the married couple, and carrying it still further—

A priest incarcerated in a Communist prison is subjected to unbelievable physical and psychological torture. On Christmas Day he begs to be allowed to say Mass. Permission is given. With awe and bliss he intones the words of the liturgy—but, horror of horrors, at the moment of the Consecration when he is about to say the holy words, the torturers gag him and shout, "This is *not* my body; this is *not* my blood!" What a diabolic desecration!

Now, here is the comparison:

It is the fertile time. There is the couple joined in sexual union: a new life can enter the world! But no! Instead, the life-giving sperm is contained in a little rubber bag, later to be discarded.

Or, perhaps even more grotesque, the woman has taken a pill which prevents conception by causing a simulated pregnant state—mocking, betraying the natural state and making real conception and child-bearing impossible. What a desecration!

I believe that the argument I have just advanced based on the sacredness of the fertile period is sufficient to show why its violation is intrinsically evil as *Humanae Vitae* states (n. 14) in language less vivid but just as insistent. Other related and important arguments against contraceptives were also advanced before or shortly after the promulgation of the encyclical; they certainly deserve greater consideration than they received at that troubled time.[23]

However, some problems remain. What about the normal physical expression of marital love? Isn't that sacred, too? Isn't any day a good time to express such love—even if, for important reasons, the couple has decided not to have more children?

To this difficulty, the basic answer of the encyclical is very clear (n. 16). In other words:

unitive sexual love without intent to procreate	corresponds to	the non-fertile time
unitive sexual love with intent to procreate	corresponds to	the fertile time

---

23. See the excellently phrased discussion in the collective pastoral letter of the U.S. Bishops, *Human Life in Our Day* (Boston: St. Paul Editions, 1968). For a fine phenomenological defense based on the importance of love, see Dietrich Von Hildebrand, *The Encyclical Humanae Vitae: A Sign of Contradiction* (Chicago: Franciscan Herald Press, 1969). For an ingenious discussion in terms of natural law, see Germain Grisez, *Contraception and the Natural Law* (Milwaukee: Bruce, 1964). An analysis in terms of the historical situation at the time of *Humanae Vitae* which also

Both experiences of love are God-given and blessed. The conformity of one's sexual life to such a natural rhythm is no more a desecration than the conformity of a farmer's planting times to the seasons of the year.

In the past, special problems arose because some couples had difficulty determining the fertile period. They thought that the rhythm method did not work and that the practical choice might be between total abstinence or yearly child-bearing. (Incidentally, it is important to realize that it is not part of the order of nature to conceive every year. The mother's body is designed for breast-feeding, which in former times lasted several years, in most cases rendering her less fertile, with a resulting natural favorable spacing of births.)

Looking back at the time just before the encyclical, the 1950's and '60's, and reviewing my own experiences, I must say that there were no lack of ambiguities connected with blaming rhythm for unwanted pregnancies. Many couples used guesswork, when more precise methods were available and known to them. How can we explain such inefficiency about a matter so important? I am convinced that it came about because the strong physical, emotional and spiritual motives behind the joys of participation and experience of the whole creative cycle often outweighed any prior considerations. Except in certain cases, the impulsive leap of faith involved in love-making at a time when fertility is possible though not probable, seems to me to be part of the family vocation. The acceptance of the extremely heavy burden of child-raising for the reward of another beloved little one is a sign of holiness. Those who regard couples having many children as objects of scorn are in my view as misguided as those who regard saintly priests, sisters and brothers as lacking in moderation when they exhaust themselves in their ministries.

---

gives very concrete arguments can be found in the book by Christopher Derrick, *Honest Love and Human Life* (New York: Coward McCann, 1969), p. 145.

Nonetheless, there certainly were instances involving heroic sacrifice, for example, if a new pregnancy would imperil the mother's health gravely and she had an irregular cycle which was hard to predict, so that almost total abstinence was required. The plight of such couples was the motive behind the hope for a change in the Church's ban on contraception. Possibly the "pill" would provide the loophole, since its use did not directly mutilate the sexual act. (Now, of course, the pill is considered to be very dangerous to health and hopefully is no longer being recommended as a solution.)

Pope Paul was aware of the sufferings of couples who could not work successfully with the rhythm method. When his final decision was made, it was with absolute conviction of reflecting the will of God, but with a heavy heart and with prayer that new methods would be discovered which would eliminate trial and error and thus insure to couples who had serious reasons for avoiding procreation more time to experience unitive sexual love.[24]

Thanks be to God, there was an answer—an accurate system discovered by two doctors (an Australian married couple), whose research began with women for whom previous methods did not work. It is called the Natural Ovulation or Billings Method. (There are booklets available on it at most Catholic bookstores and short courses for couples at hospitals.)

The discovery of this natural method is a great breakthrough. The method should be studied by every young couple. It is even being adopted purely on health grounds by people with no interest in Catholic moral teachings.

From my own personal experience with three children and five miscarriages, after each one of which doctors advised me to allow a period of one year without pregnancy, I can witness to the fact that the new method

24. See *Humanae Vitae*, nn. 24, 25.

is easy. It takes only minutes per month to calculate and usually demands no more than seven days of abstinence per month—often fewer. If with God's grace celibacy is possible, who can doubt that married couples can make such a small sacrifice? At first it may seem hard, because many women are more desirous of sexual union at the fertile time, but with practice many married people find that periodic abstinence heightens sexual enjoyment, turning the non-fertile days into little honeymoons.

Moreover, this kind of abstinence is really participation through sacrifice in the mystery of fertility—I experience it as a sort of reverent bowing before the plans that God has written into nature.

How I wish that married couples with sound theological, spiritual and psychological training would take up the idea of forming a ministry to other families in the parish, as suggested by Pope Paul in the encyclical.[25] How much we can learn from one another!

Many couples decide on contraceptives because of ignorance of new methods. Others need counseling to overcome the habit of substituting compulsive sexuality for different means of expressing love. Many women, after participation in marital renewal retreats or other spiritual exercises, have discovered that the physical coldness they felt toward their husbands was due more to resentment than to the frustration of desire at peak fertile times. Others need more teaching on parenthood, since it is the chaotic upbringing of the children whom they already have which makes them terrified of having more. Many couples make up their minds that they have grave reasons to avoid having more than two children because they think a college education is a necessity. There is a great need for value-clarification here. On the basis of such a mentality three-fourths of the people in the world are mistakes! As I often ask my students, let me ask you, the reader:

---

25. See *Humanae Vitae*, n. 26.

If your parents had the same ideas about birth control that you do now, would you have been born?

When I discuss the question of contraception with religious, the remark is often made that my views may be suitable for very spiritual people but should not be the norm for all. I must admit to being dismayed by such an attitude. If it is demanding too much to ask Catholic parents to abstain for seven days a month, how can young people be expected to hold the ideal of pre-marital purity, which is much more difficult? Of course, all of us are weak and confused at times, but the more we understand this, the more we should desire to be helped and to help others find the light, for only the truth can make us free. The truth must be preached "in season and out of season," since we must "hate the sin, and love the sinner," as Augustine wrote. In the words that the encyclical addresses to Christian husbands and wives:

"Let them implore divine assistance by persevering prayer; above all, let them draw from the source of grace and charity in the Eucharist...and if sin should keep its hold over them, let them not be discouraged, but rather have recourse with humble perseverance to the mercy of God, which is poured forth in the Sacrament of Penance."[26]

In connection with the importance of teaching the truth, it was a matter of profound interest to me to read an article by one of the leading moral theologians among the original dissenters from the encyclical.[27] In retraction, he explains that developments subsequent to the encyclical have truly revealed the dangers of the contraceptive mentality. Clearly, once sexuality is separated from reverence for fertility, the door is left open to every extreme: pre-marital, extra-marital, homosexual and mastabatory sex.

---

26. *Humanae Vitae*, n. 25.

27. See Peter Riga, "*Humanae Vitae* and the New Sexuality," *Faith*, Vol. 6, n. 3, May-June (1974), 8-11.

For many Catholics, especially younger ones, if an act is experienced as leading to "growth" or as an expression of love, that is enough to insure its goodness.

The growing tendency to rationalize sexual sin in terms of loose conscience makes it especially important to analyze formation of conscience closely with respect to the prohibition of contraception.

For example, very often the statement is made by educators and priests that since *Humanae Vitae* is only an encyclical, there is no reason to treat its concepts as certain. But *Humanae Vitae* is not the only place where the Catholic doctrine on contraception is stated:

"When it is a question of harmonizing married love with the responsible transmission of life, it is not enough to take only the good intention and the evaluation of motives into account; objective criteria must be used, criteria which respect the total meaning of mutual self-giving and human procreation.... In questions of the regulation of generation, the children of the Church, faithful to these principles, are forbidden to use methods disapproved of by the Magisterium in its interpretation of the divine law." [28]

Furthermore, consulting standard texts, I discover that the condemnation of contraception is a constant, explicit, universal teaching of the Church[29] based on natural law[30] and therefore falling under "faith and morals." What is more, I find in *Lumen Gentium* that even the ordinary teaching authority of the Church must be obeyed.[31]

---

28. *Church in the Modern World*, n. 51.

29. For an excellent short summary see John A. Hardon, *The Catholic Catechism* (Garden City, NY: Doubleday, 1975), pp. 367-381.

30. Hardon, *The Catholic Catechism*, pp. 231-232; see also *Human Life in Our Day*, and G. D. Smith, *The Teachings of the Catholic Church*, Vol. II (New York: Macmillan Co., 1949), pp. 1064, 1088-92.

31. See Vatican II, *Dogmatic Constitution on the Church* (Boston: St. Paul Editions, 1965), n. 25.

The obligation remains to inform one's conscience, so that it will not be erroneous.

Even though it is important in questions involving guilt and sin to understand that no one can be in mortal sin who is convinced that his or her choice is God's will, the application of "primacy of conscience" to questions of dissent is ambiguous.

In the cases of many people I have spoken with, it seems clear that their consciences were not certain but *wavering* until they became certain because "Fr. X" explained to them that their subjective feelings were more important than the objective norm. (I have rarely met a dissenting university graduate who had bothered to read a single defense of the encyclical before making so weighty a decision of conscience.) Of course, the lay person may often over-simplify or distort what "Fr. X" actually said. However, nowadays it is often the case that "Fr. X" himself does not think that contraception is really wrong as long as the intentions of the couple are good. It is hardly to be expected that in such a case he would be able to overturn the erroneous conscience of the married couple he is counseling with an eloquent, appealing defense of the objective norm.

Because of his own doubts about contraception "Fr. X" may be willing to leave the question up to the consciences of his penitents without giving them adequate means of forming their evaluations on the basis of Catholic teaching. But can he ignore the disquieting evidence that primacy of conscience is being invoked about other matters which he is sure are intrinsically wrong?

I have heard devout Catholics who go to Mass every day and whose fundamental option would appear to be wonderful, actually justify pre-marital, extra-marital and even homosexual union as good on the basis of the idea that love is the chief Gospel value and that holding back from physical expression may impoverish growth of relationship with others.

The reasoning of such Catholics shows how important it is to dwell on basic, objective concepts about the God-given meaning of human sexuality. In this light we can see how tremendously significant is the truth expressed in *Humanae Vitae*. Either we acknowledge sexuality and fertility as sacred gifts of God to be used by man and woman under the lordship of Christ and by Catholics in obedience to the Holy Spirit as he speaks through legitimate ministers of governance, or the miraculous power of sexuality will increasingly be seized from God—not "Thy will be done" but "my will be done!"

I pray that these reflections may be a link in the chain of affirmation of the mysteries of Christian love expressed in Catholic truth.

> "Create a pure heart in me, O God,
>   and put a new and loyal spirit in me....
> Sincerity and truth are what you require;
>   fill my mind with your wisdom....
> Give me again the joy that comes from your
>   salvation,
>   and make me willing to obey you.
> Then I will teach sinners your commands,
>   and they will turn back to you" (Psalm 51–TEV).

Homosexuality

Main Problem: In recent years due to causes psychological, sociological and moral, there has been an enormous increase in open homosexuality. There is agitation among homosexuals who consider themselves to be Christians that their lifestyle be accepted as an alternate one rather than condemned as intrinsically evil.

Scripture and Tradition:

Scripture refers to homosexual activity, masturbation, fornication with animals, etc., as unnatural, unclean acts. Passages condemning these acts include:

Genesis 19:5 ("know" = to have intercourse); Leviticus 18:6-23; 20:13; Judges 19:22; Wisdom 14:22-29; Ephesians 4:19; and the most often quoted Romans 1:24-27, 32:

"For this reason God gave them up to dishonorable passions. Their women exchanged natural relations for unnatural, and the men likewise gave up natural relations with women and were consumed with passion for one another, men committing shameless acts with men and receiving in their own persons the due penalty for their error....

"Though they know God's decree that those who do such things deserve to die, they not only do them but approve those who practice them" (Romans 1:24-27, 32).

Note that in Scripture "to know" in a sexual context means to have intercourse.

The wrongness of homosexual practices has been reaffirmed over and over again through the present day.[32]

On the other hand, having a homosexual *orientation* as opposed to *practice* is not in itself blameworthy, since many times it is rooted in psychological disorders. Growth in Christian maturity makes it possible to control such desires, and intense counseling may lead to the healing of psychological problems, especially if the person involved wants to change. As Pope Paul VI states: "The Master, who speaks with great severity in this matter [of chastity] does not propose an impossible thing (Matthew 5:28). We Christians, regenerated in baptism, though we are not freed from this kind of weakness, are given the grace to overcome it."[33]

Here ends the admittedly very brief survey of some controversial questions about what is intrinsically evil and good, unloving and loving, as explained in Scripture and Tradition.

---

32. See Hardon, *The Catholic Catechism*, p. 355, and footnote 43, p. 585.

33. Paul VI, "To Live the Paschal Mystery," address, May, 1971.

To Live in Love
Now and Forever

In this book, *Living in Love,* I have tried to show that love involves both feeling and responsibility. I believe that everyone wants to be loving, but that we are blocked by our faults and by uncertainty, often caused by selfishness.

On the basis of intuitions and reason we can determine what is loving and unloving, good and evil, but actually living in terms of the loving and good in spite of the pressure to choose selfishly, is fostered by strong belief in a God of Love.

When we know the Lord, the answer to the skeptical query, "Who's to say what's right or wrong?" becomes clear: The Lord is to say!

Knowing our tendency toward self-deception, we are happy to be part of a Church of Love. The same Church in which Christ intimately enters us out of love through his sacraments, is also the Church through which the Holy Spirit can guide us.

The original meaning of life was to image God, the Father, who is all goodness, love and holiness, by a perfect earthly life lived in union with him. After humankind's fall and the redemption, our participation in God's life takes place in union with Christ by the power of the Holy Spirit. It consists in restoring the broken image amidst terrible struggle with the powers of darkness that are without and within. We are received back into union with God in a continual cycle of fall, mercy, grace, thanksgiving and praise. Overshadowing all, we live in the promise of eternal joy as lovers of God and of his creation.

Originally created for paradise, the poor fallen human person is forever longing for happiness. How many of our vices have their deepest roots in the frantic need to grab, grasp and cling to whatever seems to promise such joy, at any cost to ourselves and others. We sell our souls to be popular—a tinsel substitute for the perfect appreciation each of us would have experienced in paradise. We strive ruthlessly to succeed, to demonstrate that we are powerful, hiding the puniness which follows the original fall. We make gods of material goods, that their glitter may distract us from our ugly, empty thoughts and schemes. And thus man becomes the victim of man.

And yet in the midst of our misery we have glimpses of the true good. God's beauty dances in his natural creations. God's goodness shines through simple, loving human gestures. And finally we fall in love with God made visible in the God-man, Jesus Christ, the Savior, who becomes total Victim in order to forgive, that henceforth no victim need feel alone and no victimizer despair.

We kneel before him: "You are the Life and the Truth, Lord: show us the Way!"

And as he departs he sends us the Holy Spirit, to teach, to give, to bring virtue and witness to fruition.

He forms us into Church as his mystical body. He comes to us in the Word. He is mysteriously yet intimately physically present in the sacraments. He is in the community of repentant sinners who still love the Savior and have before them the vision of the holy Mother of God and holy saints interceding.

And yet with all the truth and life and holiness, still we fall. We are like Peter, who could walk on the waters when his eyes were fixed on the figure of Christ but sank immediately when looking at himself. Mesmerized by our fantasies of redemption on earth, we grab and grasp and cling to what will not satisfy.

Then, like the prodigal son tasting dust and ashes, we remember our heavenly Father. Unworthy, we come to be cleansed in the Sacrament of Reconciliation. Hidden in Christ's wounds, we join hands again with our brothers and sisters at the supper of the Lamb.

We take up again the cross of being human and we struggle, groaning in prayer, to become good—that man may not be the victim of man. And in union with Christ, with the guidance and grace of the Spirit, enfolded in the maternal embrace of Mary, we persevere in spite of everything in loving God and neighbor, perhaps more purely because we know how impure we are!

And in the end we have been told:

"No eye has seen,
 no ear has heard,
no mind has conceived
 what God has prepared for those who love him."
(1 Corinthians 2:9–NIV)

To make the conclusion of Living in Love more personal for you, I suggest you write your own final statement as a short declaration or as a prayer.

ST. PAUL BOOK & MEDIA CENTERS
OPERATED BY THE DAUGHTERS OF ST. PAUL

ALASKA
750 West 5th Ave., Anchorage, AK 99501 **907-272-8183.**
CALIFORNIA
3908 Sepulveda Blvd., Culver City, CA 90230 **213-202-8144.**
1570 Fifth Ave. (at Cedar Street), San Diego, CA 92101 **619-232-1442.**
46 Geary Street, San Francisco, CA 94108 **415-781-5180.**
FLORIDA
Coral Park Shopping Center, 9808 S.W. 8 St., Miami, FL 33174
  305-559-6715; 305-559-6716.
HAWAII
1143 Bishop Street, Honolulu, HI 96813 **808-521-2731.**
ILLINOIS
172 North Michigan Ave., Chicago, IL 60601 **312-346-4228; 312-346-3240.**
LOUISIANA
423 Main Street, Baton Rouge, LA 70802 **504-343-4057; 504-336-1504.**
4403 Veterans Memorial Blvd., Metairie, LA 70006 **504-887-7631;**
  504-887-0113.
MASSACHUSETTS
50 St. Paul's Ave., Jamaica Plain, Boston, MA 02130 **617-522-8911.**
Rte. 1, 450 Providence Hwy., Dedham, MA 02026 **617-326-5385.**
MISSOURI
1001 Pine Street (at North 10th), St. Louis, MO 63101 **314-621-0346.**
NEW JERSEY
Hudson Mall, Route 440 and Communipaw Ave.,
  Jersey City, NJ 07304 **201-433-7740.**
NEW YORK
625 East 187th Street, Bronx, NY 10458 **212-584-0440.**
59 East 43rd Street, New York, NY 10017 **212-986-7580.**
78 Fort Place, Staten Island, NY 10301 **718-447-5071; 718-447-5086.**
OHIO
616 Walnut Street, Cincinnati, OH 45202 **513-421-5733.**
2105 Ontario Street (at Prospect Ave.), Cleveland, OH 44115
  216-621-9427.
PENNSYLVANIA
1719 Chestnut Street, Philadelphia, PA 19103 **215-568-2638;**
  215-864-0991.
SOUTH CAROLINA
243 King Street, Charleston, SC 29401 **803-577-0175.**
TEXAS
114 Main Plaza, San Antonio, TX 78205 **512-224-8101.**
VIRGINIA
1025 King Street, Alexandria, VA 22314 **703-549-3806.**
WASHINGTON
2301 Second Ave. (at Bell), Seattle, WA 98121 **206-441-4100.**
CANADA
3022 Dufferin Street, Toronto 395, Ontario, Canada.